TRUTH SEEKER:
MORMON SCRIPTURES & THE BIBLE

AN INTERPRETATION OF
ANOTHER TESTAMENT
OF JESUS CHRIST

WARREN M MUELLER

iUniverse LLC
Bloomington

iUniverse books may be ordered through booksellers or by contacting:

iUniverse
1663 Liberty Drive
Bloomington, IN 47403
www.iuniverse.com
1-800-Authors (1-800-288-4677)

Because of the dynamic nature of the Internet, any web addresses or links contained in this book may have changed since publication and may no longer be valid. The views expressed in this work are solely those of the author and do not necessarily reflect the views of the publisher, and the publisher hereby disclaims any responsibility for them.

Any people depicted in stock imagery provided by Thinkstock are models, and such images are being used for illustrative purposes only.
Certain stock imagery © Thinkstock.

ISBN: 978-1-4917-2306-7 (sc)
ISBN: 978-1-4917-2307-4 (e)

Library of Congress Control Number: 2014901373

Printed in the United States of America.

iUniverse rev. date: 2/7/2014

ACKNOWLEDGMENTS

Thanks to my Mormon friends who provided me with copies of their scriptures and offered their views in a respectful and helpful way. To remain in dialogue while sharing different points of view has been an exhilarating and enlightening experience. Thank you for helping me be a Truth Seeker.

FOREWORD
BY JORDAN R. JENSEN, PHD

I met Warren Mueller while teaching a professional soft skills seminar in Illinois. I did not tell my audience I was a member of *The Church of Jesus Christ of Latter-Day Saints* (a mainstream Mormon), but attentive attendees – like Warren – can usually identify enough context clues to put two-and-two together. Recognizing "the signs," Warren approached me on one of the seminar breaks to chat. After confirming his suspicion, he proceeded to tell me about his book project on Mormon Scripture. I was intrigued, and by day's end, had a copy of his manuscript with an invitation to review it and provide feedback from the perspective of an active member of the LDS Church.

I was honored to do so, and deeply impressed by the tremendous time and effort Warren had invested to read and study the *Book of Mormon*, the *Doctrine & Covenants*, and the *Pearl of Great Price* – nearly 900 pages of scripture! As I began reviewing his manuscript, I was even more impressed by the obvious integrity he was investing in his project. This was no "gotcha" endeavor; it was an honest attempt by a sincere Christian to understand mainstream Mormonism and then to compare and contrast its unique scriptural canon with the Holy Bible.

Over the course of my 2-year, full-time, voluntary missionary service in Alberta, Canada, I often "locked horns"—no, Mormons don't really have horns—with mainstream Christians on doctrinal interpretations of the Bible. In the course of these *"Bible bashes"* – as we missionaries referred to them – nothing meaningful was ever accomplished as the "Spirit of Christ" was usually replaced by the "Spirit of Contention" as both parties relied on the logic and rationale of man to prove his or her theological point.

As I experienced these various encounters, I was often frustrated over how *much* mainstream Christians *claimed* to know about my faith—and me—even though they had typically read very little – if any – of my Church's official scriptural canon or other original source material. Such persons were usually *well read* in anti-Mormon literature—including the embittered rhetoric of disgruntled ex-Mormons eager to vent their grudges against the Church, yet they saw *no* reason to bother reading the *Book of Mormon* itself.

I say these exchanges were frustrating, but I speak too lightly; they were often down right insulting, stirring raw emotions in my tender 19-year old mind, heart, and spirit. Full of the passion of youth, and eager to defend my Church, my blood would nearly boil with angst at seeing the proliferation of what was often little more than wholesale slander. Sometimes these conversations would elicit absurd behavior as well. For example, one young, Christian college student we talked to refused to shake hands with us because he was so afraid that touching a Mormon might infect him with some kind of spiritual plague. To him, I might as well have been the devil incarnate.

You can, therefore, imagine my surprise – and gratitude – when I met and became acquainted with Warren Mueller. Finally! – A mainstream Christian who was not only willing, but sincerely *eager*, to read Mormon scripture and other legitimate LDS literature in order to learn more about my faith. And to add even more to my astonishment, he wanted to write an entire book about what he learned! What an *unusual* Christian! What a *true* Christian!

While Warren's search through Mormon scripture and other

LDS literature has not led him to convert to Mormonism, and while he and I still disagree about many spiritual and other matters in this book and beyond, I can say with pleasure and thanksgiving that Warren and I have become true friends *in* Christ. No matter what our doctrinal differences are, we share a mutual respect and rejoice in our united testimony of the Resurrected Lord and our mutual conviction of the Holy Bible's divinity.

It has been almost 13 years since I completed my missionary service in Canada. With the maturity that can only come with time and experience, I see better than ever just how much in common Mormon Christians have with Protestant Christians. As we collectively observe the increasing secularization of U.S. Culture and recognize the trends toward immorality and godlessness, it is time for *all* believers in Jesus Christ to set aside our differences and unite in the common beliefs that undergird the strength and freedoms of this great land. It is time for us to stop bickering over the doctrines that divide us and reinvest that same energy in multiplying a collective force united in Christ-centered causes of faith, family, freedom, and virtue. It is Christian ideals (Mormon & Protestant) – embraced by our Founding Fathers – that will empower the United States to remain a beacon of freedom, liberty, and faith throughout the World. It is up to all of us to teach, promote, and defend these ideals.

I invite you to read Warren's book. More importantly, I invite you to follow his example of honest scholarship and Christ-like integrity in your own search for truth. One of the fundamental tenets of the LDS faith is religious freedom. In the words of the Church's founding Prophet-President, Joseph Smith, Jr.: "We claim the privilege of worshipping Almighty God according to the dictates of our own conscience, and allow all men the same privilege, let them worship how, where, or what they may" (11th Article of Faith).

The United States of America has afforded all Americans the right to pursue a relationship with Deity in our own chosen way. It is these freedoms that made it possible for my Church to be established, to grow, and despite much persecution, to eventually prosper and flourish throughout the United States and the World. In the hope of strengthening faith and freedom in this great Land, I call upon believers of Jesus Christ everywhere – regardless of your denomination – to stand together, united in the shared principles that will sustain our rights of worship, spiritually strengthen our families – the very fabric of America – and continually bolster our mutual faith in our Redeemer, whose Second Coming we collectively anticipate with gratitude and joy.

CONTENTS

PREFACE

I have been very impressed with the dedication of young Mormon men who devote themselves to missionary work as part of their spiritual growth, the majesty and purity of Mormon temples, and the powerful singing of the Mormon Tabernacle Choir. I know a few Mormons and they seem to be people of high integrity and morals. However, I have never understood much about what they believe and this sparked my curiosity. This curiosity grew even more intense after I discovered that the Bible is among the holy scriptures of this religious faith.

I have read the Bible daily and have studied it diligently for over thirty-three years. My passion to discover and share the truths of the Bible has inspired me to write six books and over twenty articles. I have taught many Sunday school and small Bible studies, served as a deacon and a Gideon in several evangelical churches. I believe the Bible is the inspired Word of God. I consider myself a born again child of God through faith in Jesus, which motivates me to seek out and be an active member of a Bible-believing church. In other words, I am a Christian who currently happens to be a member of the Presbyterian Church of America. While I have been a member of several other Christian denominations and churches, my identity has always primarily been based on my relationship with Jesus and secondarily on my religious affiliation.

As my faith has grown, I have tried to reach out and understand others who have different beliefs. This has helped me to gain new insights into the truths of the Bible while it has deepened my conviction and reverence for the beauty and depth of the written Word. *Truth Seeker: Mormon Scriptures and the Bible* is the result of my journey of discovery through the Mormon, or Latter-day Saints (LDS), Holy Scriptures and how they compare with evangelical Christian beliefs. I have elicited the help of some Latter-day Saints who have greatly helped me to clarify my thoughts and fill in gaps in my understanding. I am very grateful to them for their thoughtful responses to my questions.

I am most grateful to Dr. Jordan R. Jensen who is a lifelong, active member of The Church of Jesus Christ of Latter-day Saints. A direct descendant (3rd great grandson) of Hyrum Smith, and a third great nephew of his brother, Joseph Smith, Jr., -- the Church's first Prophet President -- Jensen's roots run deep in Mormonism, a heritage he cherishes. Dr. Jensen reviewed this book and offered many insightful comments from the perspective of a devout Mormon. I have included his comments as footnotes. My responses to Dr.Jensen's comments appear as italicized text.

Dr. Jensen was born in Monticello, Utah and raised in Utah and Arizona. He has since lived in five States and two Provinces of Canada. He is a graduate of LDS Seminary (4 year-long high school religious courses) and Institute (2 year-long college religious courses). He served a full-time 2-year mission for the LDS Church in Edmonton, Alberta, Canada from 1999-2001, and has held numerous leadership and other service positions in local congregations of the LDS Church where he has lived.

Dr. Jensen has a Bachelor's degree in English from Utah Valley University (Orem, UT) and a Doctoral degree in Education from Fielding Graduate University (Santa Barbara, CA). He is a former State Champion (high school) and All-American (college) runner. He is also an Eagle Scout -- the highest rank awarded by the Boy Scouts of America. He has authored hundreds of news and other articles as a journalist, popular writer, and blogger. He has also authored three books including *Self-Action Leadership:*

The Key to Everything -- The World's Most Comprehensive Guide to Self-Leadership (2013), *Psalms of Life: A Poetry Collection* (2012), and *I Am Sovereign: The Power of Personal Leadership* (2005). He is the founder and CEO of Freedom Focused, a training organization dedicated to Self-Leadership and other soft skills training topics. As a public speaker, he has presented professionally over 400 times throughout the United States, Canada, and the United Kingdom. He lives with his wife and son in the Houston, Texas area.

The organization of the book includes summaries of the LDS scriptures followed by my comments and those of Dr. Jensen. The chapters titled "Articles of Faith" and "Author Reflections" summarize basic Mormon religious beliefs and practices based on my review of the Brigham Young University and LDS websites. The book *This Is My Doctrine: The Development of Mormon Theology* (2011) by Dr. Charles Harrell is an important resource in the development of the Summary. This book was recommended to me by one of my Mormon friends. I have found it to be a thorough and honest evaluation of the development of Mormon theology. This book does not hold back on identifying and discussing inconsistencies in Mormon beliefs. I highly recommend it for anyone who is interested in a comprehensive critique of Mormonism by a Mormon.

Abbreviations for the books of the Bible and Mormon Scriptures are listed according to the *Book of Mormon* Index.

This book is not meant to be a theological debate but rather a dialogue between two devout Christians who are earnestly seeking truth through their holy scriptures. Therefore, the views expressed in this book do not claim to officially represent the LDS Church or The Presbyterian Church of America. Rather they are the interpretation of LDS and PCA doctrines by active members of these Churches.

OLD TESTAMENT

Gen	Genesis	2 Sam	2 Samuel	Ps	Psalm
Ex	Exodus	1 Kgs	1 Kings	Prov	Proverbs
Lev	Leviticus	2 Kgs	2 Kings	Eccl	Ecclesiastes
Num	Numbers	1 Chr	1 Chronicles	Song	Song of Solomon
Deut	Deuteronomy	2 Chr	2 Chronicles	Isa	Isaiah
Josh	Joshua	Ezra	Ezra	Jer	Jeremiah
Judg	Judges	Neh	Nehemiah	Lam	Lamentations
Ruth	Ruth	Esth	Esther	Ezek	Ezekiel
1 Sam	1 Samuel	Job	Job	Dan	Daniel
Hosea	Hosea	Joel	Joel	Amos	Amos
Obad	Obadiah	Jonah	Jonah	Micah	Micah
Nahum	Nahum	Hab	Habakkuk	Zeph	Zephaniah
Hag	Haggai	Zech	Zechariah	Mal	Malachi

NEW TESTAMENT

Matt	Matthew	Gal	Galatians	Heb	Hebrews
Mark	Mark	Eph	Ephesians	James	James
Luke	Luke	Philip	Philippians	1 Pet	1 Peter
John	John	Col	Colossians	2 Pet	2 Peter
Acts	Acts	1 Thes	1 Thessalonians	1 Jn	1 John
Rom	Romans	2 Thes	2 Thessalonians	2 Jn	2 John
1 Cor	1 Corinthians	Titus	Titus	3 Jn	3 John
2 Cor	2 Corinthians	Philem	Philemon	Jude	Jude
Rev	Revelation				

MORMON SCRIPTURES

1 Ne	1 Nephi	Hel	Helaman	Abr	Abraham
2 Ne	2 Nephi	3 Ne	3 Nephi	JS-M	Joseph Smith-Matthew
Jacob	Jacob	4 Ne	4 Nephi	JS-H	Joseph Smith-History
Enos	Enos	Morm	Mormon	A of F	Articles of Faith
Jarom	Jarom	Ether	Ether		
Omni	Omni	Moro	Moroni		
W of M	Words Of Mormon	D&C	Doctrines and Covenants		
Mosiah	Mosiah	OD	Official Declaration		
Alma	Alma	Moses	Moses		

INTRODUCTION

The Book of Mormon is a collection of 15 books, written by ancient prophet/historians, which are named for the principal author. It is an abridged translation of the record of two great civilizations that developed in Americas. The first group, known as the Jaredites, came to the American continent after God confounded the speech of mankind and scattered them following the construction of the Tower of Babel. The second group was Jewish people descended from the prophet Lehi who left Jerusalem around 600 BC. These writings were abridged and translated by a prophet named Mormon and his son Moroni. These abridged translations were inscribed in gold plates that were hidden by Moroni in the hill named Cumorah around 421 AD.

On September 21, 1823, the resurrected Moroni appeared to Joseph Smith and "instructed him relative to the ancient record and its destined translation into the English language."[1] These plates were later delivered to Joseph Smith who translated them "by the gift and power of God." Once the plates were translated, Joseph Smith gave them back to Moroni so they were never seen again. Eleven people saw the gold plates and provided written statements attesting to this.

Four different types of plates are mentioned, from which the *Book of Mormon* was translated:

---

1   Introduction to the *Book of Mormon.*

1

The Plates of Nephi—Large and small metal plates on which the history of the descendants of the prophet Nephi are recorded.

The Plates of Mormon—Abridged translation from some of the large plates of Nephi by the prophet Mormon including commentaries.

The Plates of Ether—Abridged translation of the history of the Jaredites by the prophet Mormon.

The Plates of Brass—Records brought by the people of Lehi from Jerusalem around 600 BC. These records contain the five books of Moses and the history of the Jews through the reign of King Zedekiah.

The Book of Mormon is purported to be "comparable to the Bible." Joseph Smith said that it is "the most correct of any book on earth." It is a record of God's dealings with the ancient inhabitants of the Americas and it contains "the fullness of the everlasting gospel." The Church of Jesus Christ of Latter-day Saints (LDS) is founded upon this book and its adherents are referred to informally as Mormons. The Mormons believe that their church is "the Lord's kingdom once again established on the earth preparatory to the second coming of the Messiah."

In the introduction to *The Book of Mormon*, all men everywhere are invited to read it and "to ask God, the Eternal Father, in the name of Christ if the book is true." *Truth Seeker: Mormon Scriptures & the Bible* summarizes this book as well as the *Doctrines and Covenants* and *The Pearl of Great Price* that, in concert with the Bible, constitute the scriptures recognized by Mormons.

The content of these books is reviewed for internal consistency as well as consistency with accepted historical records. Finally, the terms and concepts are compared to their historic context and the Bible. The perspectives of Mormons are included as footnotes under the Author Comment sections. My responses to Mormon comments in the footnotes are provided as italicized text following the footnotes.

The Doctrine and Covenants is a collection of divine revelations given to Joseph Smith and some of his successors in the Presidency of The Church of Jesus Christ of Latter-day Saints. Therefore, it is considered among the sacred scriptures by LDS members. Unlike *The Book of Mormon* and the *Bible*, it is not a translation of ancient documents but it is a recent work for the restoration of the kingdom of God in these latter days. *The Doctrines and Covenants* covers a wide range of subjects including the struggles to build Zion in America, translations of portions of the *Bible* and *The Book of Mormon,* and theological matters such as the nature of God, origin of man, need for repentance, the works of the Holy Spirit, future judgment, life after death and church administration.

The Pearl of Great Price is a collection of selected works of Joseph Smith first compiled in 1851 to make them available to LDS members. There have since been a number of revisions and rearrangements of the contents including moving some works to *The Doctrines and Covenants.* The present version of *The Pearl of Great Price* includes the following books:

Selections from the Book of Moses is an extract of the book of Genesis of Joseph Smith's translation of the Bible.

The Book of Abraham is a translation of Egyptian papyri by Joseph Smith containing writings of the patriarch Abraham.

Joseph Smith—Matthew is an extract of the gospel of Matthew found in Joseph Smith's translation of the Bible.

Joseph Smith—History contains excerpts from his official testimony and history recorded in the *History of the Church.*

The Articles of Faith of the Church of Jesus Christ of Latter-day Saints is a statement by Joseph Smith that together with a short history of the LDS Church were known as the Wentworth Letter.

AUTHOR COMMENTS ———————————————

The introduction begins by stating that *The Book of Mormon* is comparable to the Bible as they both contain "the fullness of the everlasting gospel." However, there is also a quote by Joseph Smith stating *The Book of Mormon* is the "most correct book of any book on earth" and that a man could get closer to God by abiding by its precepts than with any other book. These statements by Joseph Smith appear to say that *The Book of Mormon* is superior and not comparable to the Bible[2].

The Urim and Thummim mentioned in the Bible are two objects used in decision making by the high priest. What these objects were is not clear in the Bible but they were inserted into the breastplate of the high priest (Ex 28:30; Lev 8:8). Many scholars believe that the Urim and Thummim were lost when the Babylonians destroyed the first temple in Jerusalem. However, the last mention of the Urim and Thummim in the Bible is by the prophet Ezra who states that the governor ordered that certain priests be removed from the temple service until "a priest ministering with the Urim and Thummim" was found (Ezra 2:62-63). It is unclear whether the Urim and Thummim were in use or whether this was a way to exclude priests of questionable lineage from temple service after the exiles returned from Babylon.

The Book of Mormon says that two stones in silver bows fastened to a breastplate "constituted what is called the Urim and Thummim." These Urim and Thummim stones were given to Joseph Smith with the sacred plates and were used by him in the translation of the plates. Thus, the *Book of Mormon* defines the Urim and Thummim as stones set in bows. The Bible says that

---

2 Logically a book can be both superior and comparable at the same time. Comparable means similar. While it may seem sometimes that the *Book of Mormon* is postured as a superior book, the truth is the LDS Church values the two books equally. The reasons the *Book of Mormon* sometimes appears to be valued above the Bible is because it is a unique Christian document that many Christians are not familiar with and because it has not undergone multiple translations like the Bible.

they were used for decision making while the *Book of Mormon* says they were used for translating the sacred plates delivered to Joseph Smith.

In order for the true Church of Jesus Christ to once again become "operative as an institution among men" as it was in Old Testament and Apostolic times, Joseph Smith and Oliver Cowdery were ordained into various priesthoods. John the Baptist ordained them into the Aaronic Priesthood then the apostles Peter, James and John ordained them into the Melchizedek Priesthood (D&C 13; 27:12). "Other ordinations followed in which the priesthood keys were conferred on them by Moses, Elijah, Elias and many ancient prophets" (D&C 110; 128:18, 21). Based on these ordinations, the true Church of Jesus Christ was given authority "to teach the gospel and administer the ordinances of salvation" (Pearl of Great Price, JS-History 1:1–75; D&C 20).

This view of the Christian church prior to the establishment of the LDS Church appears to be one of a dysfunctional condition. In fact, the LDS Church believes that priesthood power and authority are not something to be taken but must be bestowed by God (A of F #5). Among Christian Churches, only the Roman Catholic Church claims to have such an unbroken line of authority invested in a line of persons that this Church traces back to Peter. The LDS Church claims that Christ's authorized priesthood power and authority were lost with the death of the ancient apostles and were later restored when conferred upon Joseph Smith.

The LDS Church teaches that priesthood authority must be bestowed by the laying on of hands by those who have the authority from Christ himself. Christ himself gave his authority by the laying of his own hands upon Peter, James and John. In 1829, these same three divinely appointed apostles of Jesus Christ bestowed their authority by the laying on of hands to the prophet of the restoration, Joseph Smith.

If the LDS Church view is correct, then there has not, nor is there at present, any valid priesthood outside of the LDS Church.

The implications of this are devastating for the Roman Catholic Church, which believes that saving grace is dispensed through the sacraments administered by the priests. However, those Christian Churches that believe in salvation by faith alone rely on the priesthood of believers rather than special priests and would not be greatly affected (1 Pet 2:5).

The key requirement for authority of the priesthood for both the LDS and Roman Catholic Church rests upon divine delegation from the apostles. Both of these churches believe that this authority can only be conveyed by the laying on of hands. I find no evidence in the Bible that suggests that Jesus laid his hands on his apostles to empower them. It is true that the apostles and elders laid their hands to commission others (Acts 6:6; 13:3). Jesus did breathe on his disciples and said "If you forgive anyone his sins, they are forgiven; if you do not forgive them, they are not forgiven" (John 20:23). This appears to me to be the best Biblical evidence for the transferal of power and authority from Jesus to the apostles but I am not aware of any churches practicing this method!

THE FIRST BOOK OF NEPHI

In the first year of the reign of King Zedekiah, the Jewish prophet Nephi wrote that his father Lehi had a vision of heaven. Lehi was given a book by a person who descended from heaven. In it, he read of the abominations and desolations of Jerusalem. These evil practices would cause God to judge his people and many of them would be taken captive to Babylon if they refused to repent. Having seen and read many marvelous things in the vision, Lehi praises God and writes many things, some of which Nephi records on metal plates.

Lehi prophesies to the Jews about their wickedness and destruction as well as "the coming of a Messiah and the redemption of the world" (1 Ne 1:19). The Jews become angry and reject him. Lehi takes his family into the wilderness after being warned in a dream that the Jews are planning to kill him. Lehi's family consists of his wife Sariah and their sons Laman, Lemuel, Sam, and Nephi. After they reach the borders of the Red Sea, the eldest sons (Laman and Lemuel) complain against their father. They do not believe that Jerusalem will be destroyed. Nephi believes his father and convinces his brother Sam. Nephi prays for Laman and Lemuel.

God speaks to Nephi and blesses him saying that, because of his faith, he would be a ruler and teacher over his brothers. Furthermore, God promises to lead Nephi to a "land which is choice above all other lands" (1 Ne 2:20).

Lehi has a dream and tells Nephi to return to Jerusalem in

order to obtain a record of the Jews written on brass plates in the home of a relative named Laban. Nephi and his brothers visit Laban but are denied the plates and flee for their lives. The older brothers beat Nephi and Sam for trying to get the plates. An angel of the Lord rebukes the older brothers and tells them that Nephi will rule over them. The angel orders them to return to Jerusalem but Laman and Lemuel object saying that Laban will kill them.

Nephi persuades his brothers to return to Jerusalem. Nephi arrives at Laban's house and finds him drunk and asleep. Nephi draws Laban's sword and kills him. Nephi puts on Laban's clothes and commands his servant Zoram to accompany him with the brass plates. Zoram discovers that Nephi is not his master when they meet Nephi's brothers. Zoram agrees to go with them into the wilderness. The brass plates contain the five books of Moses and a record of the Jews to the reign of King Zedekiah. Lehi finds his genealogy on the plates and discovers that he is a descendent of Joseph.

The Lord commands Nephi and his brothers to return to Jerusalem to bring Ishmael and his family into the wilderness. Ishmael and his family go with Nephi to the tent of Lehi in the wilderness. On their way, Laman and Lemuel, along with two sons and two daughters of Ishmael rebel and wish to return to Jerusalem. Nephi tries to persuade them to stay but they bind him and leave him in the wilderness. Nephi prays to God for deliverance. God strengthens Nephi and he breaks the bonds. Laman and Lemuel are persuaded to continue the journey into the wilderness and arrive at the tent of Lehi.

Lehi has a vision in which he partakes of a white fruit from a tree in a large field. He is filled with joy and sees a river near the tree. His wife Sariah, Nephi and Sam also partake of the fruit. However, Laman and Lemuel refuse to eat the fruit. Lehi sees many people approaching on a path that leads to the tree until a "mist of darkness" surrounds them and they wander off the path and are lost. (1 Ne 8:23). Others follow a rod of iron along the path and follow it to the tree where they partake of the fruit. Lehi sees a great and spacious building on the other side of the river filled with people who mock those who eat the fruit. Some who follow the rod and taste the fruit are afterwards ashamed, fall away into forbidden paths, and are lost.

Nephi makes two sets of plates. The larger ones contain the history of his people and the smaller ones certain sacred things. Nephi tells of Lehi's dream about the destruction of Jerusalem and the exile of the Jews to Babylon. Six hundred years later the Messiah will appear. He says a prophet will come before the Messiah to "prepare the way of the Lord and make his paths straight" (1 Ne 10:8). This prophet will baptize the Messiah with water and bear witness that the Messiah is the Lamb of God who takes away the sins of the world. He also says that the Jews will slay the Messiah but he will rise from the dead. Afterwards the gospel will be proclaimed to the Gentiles.

Nephi has a vision of the Son of God descending from heaven. The Spirit of the Lord speaks to Nephi and he sees the mother of God in Nazareth who bears "the Lamb of God, yea, even the Son of the Eternal Father!" (1 Ne 11:21). Nephi sees the same tree that Lehi saw and is told that its fruit represents the love of God. He also sees the rod of iron and is told it is the Word of God, which leads to the tree of life.

Nephi also sees a prophet who prepares the way before the Messiah. When this prophet baptizes the Lamb of God, the heavens open and the Holy Ghost comes down from heaven in the form of a dove. Nephi sees the twelve disciples of the Lamb of God. The Lamb of God performs many miracles before he is slain upon the cross for the sins of the world.

Nephi has a vision of widespread destruction of mountains, plains and many cities. The Lamb of God then descends from heaven to visit his followers after his death and resurrection in Jerusalem. He sees the Holy Ghost falling on the twelve apostles who will eventually judge the twelve tribes of Israel.

An angel of God tells him the filthy water that Lehi saw in his vision is the depths of hell. Furthermore, the mists of darkness "are the temptations of the devil" while the spacious building is the "vain imaginations and the pride of the children of men" (1 Ne 12:17–18). The descendants of Nephi's brothers gather together and war against his descendants. Nephi's descendants are defeated. His brother's descendants "dwindle in unbelief" becoming a filthy and loathsome people.

Nephi sees the formation of a powerful Gentile church that tortures and kills the saints of God. Some Gentiles flee captivity across many waters and arrive in the Promised Land where they prosper and scatter the descendants of Nephi. A book that contains the fullness of the gospel goes forth from the Jews to the Gentiles but it is changed by the great and abominable church. This results in blindness that enables Satan to cause many to stumble. However, the Lamb of God will manifest himself to the Jews. Books that contain the gospel shall be delivered to the Gentiles who, with a remnant of Jews, shall convince the scattered Jews that the records of the prophets and the twelve apostles and the Lamb are true. These records shall "make known to all kindreds, tongues and peoples that the Lamb of God is the Son of the Eternal Father, and the Savior of the world; and that all men must come to him or they cannot be saved" (1 Ne 13:40).

An angel tells Nephi that those Gentiles that repent and believe in the Lamb of God will be blessed but those who do not will be destroyed. Those who believe are of the church of the Lamb of God while those who do not believe belong to the great abominable church founded by the devil. The saints of God are the church of the Lamb and are few compared to the multitudes of the abominable church. The power of the Lamb descends upon the saints in great glory. The wrath of God is poured out on the abominable church and there are wars and rumors of wars among all the nations. The angel points out a man dressed in a white robe who is said to be an apostle and who will write concerning the end of the world. Nephi is told that this apostle is called John.

Nephi's vision ends and he returns to the tent of Lehi. He finds his brothers arguing over the meaning of Lehi's vision of the olive tree and the Gentiles. Nephi explains that the olive tree represents the house of Israel and that they are a branch broken off from the tree. The fullness of the gospel of the Messiah will come to the Gentiles and from them to the seed of Lehi. When this happens, their descendants will come to know the gospel of their Redeemer and how to be saved. They shall be grafted into the olive tree but first they will be scattered by the Gentiles.

All of the Jews shall be restored "in the latter days" (1 Ne 15:19). Nephi tells his brothers about the tree of life, the rod of iron, and the river seen in Lehi's dream. He says that God will divide the wicked from the righteous based on their works. The righteous will enter the kingdom of God but the wicked shall be cast into hell.

Nephi and his brothers marry daughters of Ishmael. Lehi finds a ball of curious workmanship made of brass outside of his tent. This ball leads them into the wilderness near the Red Sea. Laman and Lemuel along with the sons of Ishmael complain about their sufferings in the wilderness. The voice of the Lord speaks to Lehi and tells him to read what is written on the ball. This causes Lehi to "tremble exceedingly." The words on the ball change "according to the faith and diligence which we gave to it" (1 Ne 16:29).

Ishmael dies and is buried in a place called Nahom. Laman stirs up Lemuel and the sons of Ishmael against Nephi and Lehi to kill them but the voice of the Lord chastens them. They continue their journey in the wilderness for eight years and arrive at a sea they name Irreantum. The Lord speaks to Nephi and tells him to build a ship. His brothers criticize Nephi calling him a fool for trying to build a ship. Nephi recalls the rebellious acts of the Israelites in Egypt and with Moses. He tells his brothers that they are rebelling against God by complaining about their hardships in the wilderness. His brothers react by wanting to kill Nephi but he warns them not to touch him. Nephi says that he is filled with the power of God and that they would wither as a dried reed if they touch him. God tells Nephi to reach out his hand and touch his brothers to shock and shake them by the power of God inside him. Nephi does this and they are shaken such that they fall before Nephi and want to worship him but he forbids it.

Nephi builds the ship not as men would do so but rather as God directs him. The families of Nephi and his brothers as well as those of Ishmael's family enter the ship. They sail towards the Promised Land. After many days, Nephi's brothers and the sons of Ishmael begin to act merry with rudeness. Nephi tries to correct them but they become angry and bind him. A great storm arises and, after four days, Nephi's brothers realize that the judgment of God is upon them. They loosen Nephi's bonds and he prays to God. The storm ceases and Nephi guides the ship to the Promised Land (with the aid of the brass ball) where they plant seeds and reap in abundance. They find many animals in the forest including cows, oxen, horses, goats, and donkeys. They also find much gold, silver, and copper (1 Ne 18:25).

Nephi makes "plates of ore" and engraves the record of his father and their journey in the wilderness. He also records his prophecies and those of Lehi. These plates were to be kept for "the instruction of my people, who should possess the land and for other wise purposes" (1 Ne 19:1–3). Nephi predicts that the God of Israel will come six hundred years after Lehi leaves Jerusalem and that he will be scourged, smitten, spit upon, and crucified. The people of Jerusalem will be persecuted by all people because they crucified the God of Israel. They will be scattered among the nations where they will be despised.

However, the day will come when they will turn their hearts toward the Holy One of Israel. Then they shall be gathered from the four corners of the earth and all the peoples of the world shall be blessed. The Lord shall be a light to the Gentiles and bring salvation to the ends of the earth. Rulers shall worship the Lord, the Redeemer of Israel. The house of Israel shall be gathered and delivered from oppression.

Nephi explains that the tribes of Israel will be scattered because they rejected the Holy One of Israel. The Lord God of Israel will "raise up a mighty nation among the Gentiles and by them shall the Jews be scattered" (1 Ne 22:7). However, they shall be gathered again to the lands of their inheritance and they shall know the Lord as their Savior. Then the great and abominable church will turn upon itself and "they shall be drunken with their own blood" (1 Ne 22:13). All those who fight against the House of Israel shall be turned against each other and destroyed. Satan shall no longer have power over the hearts of men. The wrath of God shall be poured out upon the children of men and the wicked shall perish by fire. Any who do not listen to the Holy One of Israel shall be destroyed. The Holy One of Israel shall gather his people and reign on the earth. Nephi concludes by saying that those who obey the commandments and endure to the end shall be saved.

AUTHOR COMMENTS

The word "church" refers to groups of Christian believers and religious denominations. This word first appears in the Bible in statements made by Jesus (Matt 16:18; 18–17). It appears many times in the first book of Nephi in reference to the brethren of Laban and a future abominable church that "slayeth the saints of God" (1 Ne 4:26; 13:5). Thus, the concept and usage of the word "church" are not consistent with other historic records since the first book of Nephi was written by the prophet Nephi around 600 BC.[3]

The term Lamb of God in the Bible is first used to refer to Jesus by John the Baptist. However, Nephi refers to the Messiah as the

---

3 This may be explained by the fact that Joseph Smith was translating the records into 1820s English when the word "church" was very much in use.

Lamb of God and to the apostles of the Lamb six hundred and thirty years earlier.

Nephi predicts that the Messiah and Savior of the world would appear six hundred years after Lehi's departure from Jerusalem. This is a very precise prediction that is unmatched by all the Messianic prophecies of the Old Testament. Nephi also predicts that a prophet would come "to prepare the way of the Lord." This prophet "will cry in the wilderness: Prepare ye the way of the Lord, and make his paths straight; for there standeth one among you whom ye know not; and he is mightier than I, whose shoe latchet I am not worthy to unloose" (1 Ne 10:7–8). Part of this prophecy is found in Is 40:3. However, it is much more precise than Isaiah or any of the Old Testament prophecies in that it predicts what John the Baptist will say (Luke 3:16; John 1:26).[4]

While it is true that the Bible and Book Of Mormon (BOM) agree on the redemptive mission of Jesus (i.e., his atoning death, resurrection, and ascension), there are many differences that do supplant and negate portions of the Bible. This is evident in the numerous inconsistencies and conflicts with the Bible presented in this book.

Nephi predicts that the prophet would baptize the Messiah with water and "bear record that he had baptized the Lamb of God, who should take the sins of the world." This prophecy is precisely what John the Baptist said and did as recorded in John 1:29–31.

Nephi predicts that, when the Lamb of God is baptized, the heavens will open and the Holy Ghost will come down from heaven in the form of a dove and rest upon him. This prophecy is fulfilled in the gospel accounts of the baptism of Jesus (Luke 3:21–22; John 1–32–34; Matt 3:16). Nephi also predicts that there

---

4   This is but one great value of the BOM. It is not meant to supplant or negate the Bible, but to strengthen its message of all things Christ-focused. A big misnomer among many Christians is that the BOM somehow replaces the Bible. Nothing could be further from the truth. The BOM actually makes the Bible appear all the more credible.

will initially be twelve apostles and that the Lamb of God will be crucified for the sins of the world.

These prophesies of Nephi are incredibly accurate and are much more precise that those found in the Old Testament books of the Bible. Thus, they are either superior to the Messianic prophecies of the Bible or they reflect the historic perspective of someone who wrote them well after these events occurred.[5]

The quick revelation and production of the Book of Mormon is a remarkable feat and could suggest that he had superhuman assistance. However, to be fair, we must admit that such assistance could have been demonic rather than divine. Another plausible explanation is that the Book of Mormon could have been largely written by someone else and that Joseph Smith edited it. This theory is presented in detail in the book, **Who Really Wrote the Book of Mormon** *by Wayne Cowdery et al. (2005) a descendant of Oliver Cowdery. The premise of this book is that the BOM was derived from an historic fictional novel written by a Reverend Solomon Spalding prior to the War of 1812. This book, Manuscript Found, describes how the American Indians are descended from Jewish immigrants. According to the historic research in this book, Manuscript Found, was delivered to a printer by Mr. Spalding but never published due to subsequent health and business failures. This book allegedly languished at the print shop until it was found by Reverend Sidney Rigdon who was one of the founding fathers of Mormonism.*

According to the testimony of witnesses speaking from personal knowledge, when The Book of Mormon was published in early 1830, "its narrative followed precisely the lines of Spalding's novel. The plot was the same, the exact language was, in many instances...the same, and the only

---

5   Excellently insightful observation. The truthfulness of Mormon doctrine rises or falls with the question of the veracity of the BOM. Either Joseph Smith was a prophet of God and the BOM is true or he is an imposter and the BOM and LDS Church are a sham. This is a fundamental issue that every serious investigator of Mormonism must confront. Food for thought: Could a 21–24 year old farm boy with a third grade formal education have done what Joseph Smith did all on his own in a total working period of only about 60 days without divine assistance?

noticeable change was the addition of scriptural passages and religious matter which did not appear in Spalding's original work" (Sewickley, PA Herald).

Nephi recounts one of the judgments of God on the Israelites because of their iniquity. This happened while they wandered in the wilderness after leaving Egypt. Nephi says that God sent "flying serpents" among them and that many died when they were bitten. (1 Ne 17:41). This story parallels the Bible accounts of Numbers 21:6 and Deuteronomy 8:15. However, the serpents of Numbers and Deuteronomy were ordinary and did not fly.

When Nephi reaches the Promised Land, he says that "there were beasts in the forests of every kind, both the cow and the ox, and the ass and the horse, and the goat" (1 Ne 18:25). The problem with this statement is that there were no horses or goats in the Americas around 600 BC. These animals were first introduced by Spanish settlers and explorers in the 16th century AD. Likewise, cattle and oxen were first introduced to the American continent by the Pilgrims in the 17th century AD.

LDS scholar Robert R Bennett argues that the absence of fossil evidence for horses in America prior to European colonization does not prove that there were none. He argues that there is no fossil evidence to support the fact that a large population of horses was used by the Huns.[6]

---

6   [8] http://maxwellinstitute.byu.edu/publications/transcripts/?id-129

THE SECOND BOOK OF NEPHI

Lehi speaks to his family and those with them. He says that the Promised Land shall be a "land of liberty" to those who follow the commands of God (2 Ne 1:7). They shall prosper and the land shall be kept from all other nations. However, they will dwindle in unbelief after receiving great blessings. They will reject the Messiah and then other nations shall come to take away their land. Lehi prays that his people will avoid God's wrath by observing the statutes of God. He tells them to "put on the armor of righteousness" and not to rebel against Nephi (2 Ne 1:23). Lehi offers his blessings if his sons listen to Nephi.

Lehi says that redemption comes through the Messiah who will offer himself as a sacrifice for sin. The Messiah will lay down his life and take it up again to become the first of those who rise from the dead. Those who believe in him shall be saved.

Lehi tells of the fall of the devil and Adam and Eve. If Adam and Eve had not sinned, they would have remained in the Garden of Eden without children as they would have remained in a state of innocence. Because of the fall, mankind is free to choose eternal life or death and has the potential to become like the Heavenly Father (2 Ne 2:22–25).

Lehi blesses Joseph, who is his youngest son, and says that his descendants will not be destroyed. A great prophet like Moses will be among Joseph's descendants. This prophet shall be named

Joseph.[7] After Lehi finishes his prophecies concerning Joseph, he calls his children together. He blesses them and says, "because of my blessing the Lord God will not suffer that ye shall perish; wherefore, he will be merciful unto you and unto your seed forever." Lehi dies shortly thereafter and is buried.

Nephi prays for deliverance from evil without and within himself. He asks for guidance and places his trust in God. Nephi's brothers turn against him and seek to kill him because they reject him as having God's authority to rule over them. Nephi takes his family (as well as those of others who believe in his revelations from God) into the wilderness to separate themselves from the Lamanites. They settle in a place they name Nephi and call themselves Nephites. They follow the commandments of God and prosper. Nephi takes the sword of Laban and makes others like it to defend themselves against the Lamanites.

The Nephites build a temple similar to Solomon's but not as glorious. The people desire Nephi to be their king but he refuses saying they should not have a king. The Lamanites, who are Lehi's descendants that did not follow Nephi, are cursed by God because of their disobedience. Their skin turns from white to black so "that they might not be enticing to the Nephites" (2 Ne 5:21). God curses any intermarriage between the two groups of people.

Jacob and Joseph are consecrated as priests by Nephi. Forty years have passed since their departure from Jerusalem. The Lamanites and the Nephites have wars and contentions.

Jacob reads to the Nephites from the book of Isaiah. He says that the words of Isaiah spoken to the Jews are also for the Nephites. Jacob says that Jerusalem has fallen and those within have been carried away as captives. However, the Jews shall return and afterwards the Lord God will appear to them in the

---

7 The original Joseph of Egypt in Biblical times also prophesied of Joseph Smith in a parallel way that Lehi did. This was one of the "plain and precious" truths that was lost from original Bible transcripts. It appears toward the end of the Joseph Smith translation of the Book of Genesis.

flesh. The Jews will scourge and crucify him. As a result, they will be scattered and hated but they will be gathered to the "lands of their inheritance" after they "come to the knowledge of their Redeemer" (2 Ne 6:11). The Messiah shall return in power and great glory. Those who do not believe in him shall be destroyed and "know that the Lord is God, the Holy One of Israel" (2 Ne 6:15).

The Lord shall comfort Zion and restore his people. The Jews will be restored "to the true church" when they are gathered to "the lands of their inheritance" (2 Ne 9:2). The Creator will come in the flesh and suffer and die for all men as an infinite atonement for their sins. The death of the Holy One of Israel provides a way for mankind to escape death and hell.

God will judge everyone. Those who believe in the Holy One of Israel shall inherit the kingdom of God. Those who do not believe shall be cast into hell where there is endless torment in a lake of fire and brimstone. God commands that all men must repent, be baptized in his name and have "perfect faith in the Holy One of Israel, or they cannot be saved in the kingdom of God" (2 Ne 9:23).

Jacob pleads for his brethren to turn away from their sins and "come unto that God who is the rock of your salvation" (2 Ne 9:45). Christ will be crucified by the Jews because of "priest crafts and iniquities" (2 Ne 10:5). The Jews shall be scattered among the nations until they are re-gathered to the lands of their inheritance.

Nephi writes the words of Isaiah concerning the establishment of the Lord's house. God will judge the nations and they shall "beat their swords into plowshares and their spears into pruning hooks" (2 Ne 12:4). The day of the Lord shall come when God alone shall be exalted and man shall be bowed low. The Jews and Jerusalem shall be punished and purged of evil.

In the year that King Uzziah dies, Isaiah sees the Lord on a throne surrounded by angels with six wings. One of the angels takes a burning coal in his hand and places it in Isaiah's mouth saying, "Lo, this has touched thy lips; and thine iniquity is taken away, and thy sin purged" (2 Ne 16:7). God commands Isaiah to speak his words to the Jews until the cities are wasted and the land is desolate.

Immanuel shall be born of a virgin. The Lord of Hosts shall be a stone of stumbling and a rock of offense to Israel. A child shall be born "and the government shall be upon his shoulder; and his name shall be called, Wonderful, Counselor, The Mighty Father, the Prince of Peace" (2 Ne 19:6).

God shall punish the king of Assyria because of his pride. The Lord shall "smite the earth with the rod of his mouth, and with the breath of this lips shall he slay the wicked" (2 Ne 21:4). The earth shall be at peace, the wolf shall dwell with the lamb, and the lion shall eat straw like the ox. The earth shall be full of the knowledge of the Lord. The Lord will gather for the second time a remnant of his people from the four corners of the earth and God will dwell among his people.

In the day of the Lord, sinners will be destroyed and the stars will not shine. The sun and moon will be dark. The heavens will be shaken and the earth will move from its place. Babylon shall become desolate like Sodom and Gomorrah. Satyrs and dragons shall inhabit their desolate dwellings. Lucifer shall be cast out of heaven into hell.

Jerusalem shall be destroyed and the Jews scattered after the departure of Lehi. They will be carried away as captives to Babylon. God will restore the captive Jews to the land of their inheritance. Thereafter, the Only Begotten of the Father will appear in the flesh. The Jews shall crucify him and, after he is laid in a grave for three days, he will rise from the dead. "All those who shall believe on his name shall be saved in the kingdom of God" (2 Ne 25:13). Jerusalem will be destroyed a second time after the Messiah is risen from the dead. The Jews will be scattered among the nations for many generations.

The Messiah will come six hundred years after Lehi leaves Jerusalem. The name of the Messiah shall be Jesus Christ the Son of God. There is no other name given under heaven except for Jesus Christ by which men can be saved. Therefore, belief in Christ is taught to persuade Nephi's brethren and children so they can be reconciled to God. Nephi says that it is "by grace that we are saved, after all we can do" (2 Ne 25:23). He continues by saying that believers have become dead to the Law of Moses and are alive in Christ because of faith. Nevertheless, "we keep the law because of the commandments." Therefore, believe in Christ, who is the Holy One of Israel, and keep the Law of Moses.

Christ shall appear to the Nephites after his resurrection. They shall have peace until many of the fourth generation have died and then they will be destroyed. Those who have dwindled in unbelief will be smitten by the Gentiles. Many churches shall be built by the Gentiles and there shall be priest crafts. These priest crafts are evil because "they set themselves up for a light unto the world, that they may get gain and praise from the world; but they do not seek the welfare of Zion" (2 Ne 26:29). God has commanded that man should not murder, lie, steal, swear, envy, be contentious, or commit immoral sexual acts.

In the last days, evil shall abound in the earth. The Lord of Hosts shall come with thunder, earthquakes, great noise, storms, and devouring fire. God will bring forth a book that will be delivered to one man and witnessed by three. Some of the words of this book will be sealed and cannot be read until God decides to reveal them. Many churches shall arise and claim to be true to the Lord. Their priests shall contend with each other and deny the Holy Ghost claiming that God has completed his work and has given his power to men. Because of their pride and false teachings, their churches have become corrupt. They rob the poor to build grand churches and provide themselves with fine clothing. Cursed is anyone who puts his faith in men and says that they have received all they need of God's Word. The great and abominable church shall fall but those who repent and return to God shall be saved.

Many Gentiles shall say "A Bible! A Bible! We have got a Bible, and there cannot be any more Bible" (2 Ne 29:3). Just because you have a Bible, do not suppose that it contains all God's words. The Jews, Nephites, and lost tribes of Israel shall be given the words of God.

Nephi tells his brethren that they must keep the commandments of God or they will perish. Those Gentiles who repent and believe in God's Son, the Holy One of Israel, shall be saved. The Gentiles shall carry the gospel of Jesus Christ to the descendants of the Nephites. The Jews that were scattered shall begin to believe in Christ and become a "delightsome people" (2 Ne 30:7). God shall work among all the nations to bring about the restoration of his people. He shall smite the earth with the rod of his mouth and slay the wicked with the breath of his lips. Then the wolf will dwell with the lamb, the lion shall eat straw like the ox and a little child will lead them. The knowledge of the Lord shall cover the earth as the waters cover the seas. All things shall then be made known to the children of men and Satan shall no longer have power over them for a long time.

Nephi says that, if the Lamb of God needed to be baptized to fulfill all righteousness, then sinful mankind has an even greater need to do so. At the baptism of Jesus, the Holy Ghost descends upon the Lord in the form of a dove. Jesus has set an example for us to follow to keep the commandments of the Father. The voice of the Son of God tells Nephi "He that is baptized in my name, to him will the Father give the Holy Ghost" (2 Ne 31:12). He also tells Nephi to "follow me and do the things which ye have seen me do." Those who are baptized in the name of Jesus with water will receive a second baptism of the Holy Ghost and will speak with "the tongue of angels" (2 Ne 31:13). Nephi says that it would be better to have not known Jesus than to deny him after being baptized and receiving the Holy Ghost. No man can be saved unless he "shall endure to the end in following the example of the Son of the living God" (2 Ne 31:16). Mankind enters the gate to eternal life by repentance and baptism. This is followed by the forgiveness of sins by "fire and by the Holy Ghost" (2 Ne 31:17). These put a man on the straight and narrow path that leads to eternal life. Nephi says that only those who "press forward, feasting upon the word of Christ and endure to the end" shall have eternal life (2 Ne 31:20). There is no other way or name given under heaven whereby men can be saved. This is "the only and true doctrine of the Father, and of the Son and of the Holy Ghost" (2 Ne 31:21). Nephi tells his brethren to pray always and to pray to the Father in the name of Christ before doing works for the Lord. Those who believe in Christ will believe Nephi's words for "they are the words of Christ" (2 Ne 33:10).

AUTHOR COMMENTS

The phrase "armor of righteousness" found in 2 Nephi 1:23 is only found in the Bible in 2 Corinthians 6:7, although there is a similar concept in Ephesians 6:11–13. The apostle Paul uses this idea when he speaks of God's provision for believers to wage spiritual warfare in spreading the gospel of Christ. Lehi uses this phrase to exhort his descendants to cast off the spiritual bondage that keeps them from following the commandments of God. Lehi calls this bondage "the sleep of hell" that binds men so that they are "carried away captive down to the eternal gulf of misery and woe" (2 Ne 1:13). Thus, both the Bible and 2 Nephi have similar concepts regarding provisions by God to enable his people to resist the attacks of demons. In the Bible, these ideas are not fully developed or expressed in the manner that Lehi does until the apostle Paul pens them some 650 years later. Therefore, we again see that, either the prophet Lehi is far advanced compared to his contemporary Old Testament prophets, or the author of this book is writing from a perspective that is familiar with the writings of Paul. [8]

---

8 It is not likely that Lehi is far advanced compared to other Old Testament prophets. However, he may have included things that Bible prophets did not or

Lehi says that "salvation is free" and that "by the law no flesh is justified" (2 Ne 2:4-5). Furthermore, it is by faith in the Messiah and his grace and mercy that men "can dwell in the presence of God" (2 Ne 2:8-9). These verses seem to agree with those of the Bible that speak of salvation by faith in Jesus by the grace of God, which is not related to good works. (Rom 6:23; Eph 2:8-9; John 3:16). However, Nephi also says that it is essential to repent, be baptized and to have "perfect faith and to endure to the end" in order to be saved. (2 Ne 9:23-24). Nephi says that a man cannot be saved unless there is repentance for sins, faith in Jesus Christ, baptism with water, baptism with the Holy Ghost and persistence to the end in keeping the commandments of God and doing good works. (2 Ne 31:13-20). According to Nephi, those who believe in Jesus and are baptized by water and the Holy Ghost have entered "a narrow path that leads to eternal life" (2 Ne 31:18). However, they cannot be saved without following the example of the Son of the Living God. (2 Ne 31:16). These passages contradict the Bible and earlier verses in 2 Nephi that say that faith in Jesus is sufficient for eternal life.[9]

The role of faith and works in salvation is best understood as faith enables you to become forgiven. When this happens, a person becomes a child of God or new creation in Christ. This is purely a legal transaction resulting from faith in Jesus Christ as personal savior. The penalty of death required as a result of sins is paid by the death of Jesus on the cross for those who believe in him. This new state of being or spiritual birth causes a change in thinking and behavior that results in doing good works as expressions of love and obedience to God who dwells within as

such details are among "the plan and precious truths" lost from the original Bible manuscripts.

9   Not so. The Bible also has seemingly contradictory verbiage as well (e.g., "by grace alone are we saved lest a man should boast" and "faith without works is dead being alone.") One must not ignore the reality that truth is often paradoxical (e.g., "whosoever shall save his life shall lose it..."). The faith versus works debate fails to take into account the element of paradoxical veracity, which validates seemingly contradictory points simultaneously.

the Holy Ghost. Thus, the Bible is not paradoxical regarding the role of faith and works in salvation. Works result from saving faith and are not part of attaining it. Some Christian denominations have caused confusion by insisting that works such as baptism are essential for salvation. This is clearly not the case as illustrated by the thief on the cross and is an error that has caused much confusion. Furthermore, Jesus says that his disciples are to take up their cross daily, to be holy and to lose their lives to find true life (Matt 16:24-25; 1 Pet 1:15). These verses are clearly impossible to accomplish by human will or effort and can only be done as God transforms the thinking and being of each believer. Miles Stanford writes on Page175 in his book **The Complete Green Letters:** "We are not to know the Lord Jesus in order to emulate Him as our example. Rather we are to behold Him in the Word and allow the Spirit of God to conform us to His image. Not imitation, but conformation."

The cross is the only way to be saved and the only way to grow spiritually in Christ (Gal 2:20). Our role is to believe and receive. We are the clay and God is the potter. The active role in transforming the clay is the work of the potter. The experience of the presence and work of God within will transform us into the likeness of Christ and enable us to do the works of God out of our new nature.

Mormons tend to emphasize the commandments as things to do in contrast to the Christian view of following the commandments as an outgrowth of faith in Christ. While both promote the importance of doing good works, I believe error occurs when doing such good works are required to assure, prove or otherwise progress in a process of either becoming a child of God or progressing as one.[10] Once this line is crossed, religious

---

10   The purpose of works is not to "assure" ourselves, or "prove" anything to God. Rather, they serve as indispensible ingredients of natural progression. To illustrate: All the Grace in the Universe won't create a bumper crop if a farmer doesn't get off the couch to plant any seeds. On the other hand, a farmer can work 24-7 cultivating his fields, but he won't get *any* crop without the sunshine and the rain. Sunshine and rain are like *Christ's Grace* – our works are meaningless without *It*, Sunshine and rain, however, aren't going to go and plant the farmer's seeds for him. Likewise, Christ's Grace will override the God-given *will* of an

ordinances such as the sacraments and going to church tend to become the goal rather than an outcome of spiritual identity and growth.[11] This reflects a thought process of doing something to become something. The Bible teaches just the opposite. A person must be born again, or spiritually born by faith in Jesus Christ alone, which results in becoming a child of God (John 1:12–13). Doing good works is an outcome of being different through the transformation of the mind by the indwelling Holy Spirit (1Cor 19–20; Rom 12:1–2). Therefore, be to do not do to be is the way to please and obey God.

Nephi says that, if Adam and Eve had not sinned, they would have remained in the Garden of Eden. In addition, everything in creation would have remained as it was created and Adam and Eve would not have had any children remaining in a state of innocence without joy since they would not have known misery. (2 Ne 2:22–23). In Genesis 1:28, God tells Adam and Eve to be fruitful and increase in number, fill the earth and subdue it. Since this happened before the fall, it implies that Adam and Eve had sexual relations before the fall.[12] In addition, filling and subduing the earth implies that God commanded them to assert control, which would change the original state in which everything was created.

---

individual who refuses salvation. Even Protestants must *do* something (viz. accept Christ) in order to obtain their version of salvation.

11   This is an astute observation because culturally speaking, it is true that Mormons can sometimes put *too* much emphasis on "checking the commandment boxes" rather than focusing on the spiritual component of obedience and one's personal relationship with Christ. It is important to note, however, that this is a cultural, not a doctrinal, phenomenon, and tends to occur among members with limited doctrinal knowledge and/or spiritual maturity. Mormon doctrine is squarely rooted in one's relationship with Christ in an effort to gradually *become* more like Him through a combination of one's own Grace empowered efforts to love Him by keeping His Commandments (*see* John 14:15 and 1 Nephi 25:23, 26).

12   Not necessarily. It just means they had to partake of the fruit of progress into full mortality where they could have children. Mormons do not view the fall as a negative event, but as a necessary step making possible Adam and Eve's eternal progression and, by default, all of ours.

God puts Adam in the garden to work and take care of it (Gen 1:15). This infers that Adam caused changes in the initial state of the Garden perhaps by gathering or cultivating plants since he was created to "work the ground" (Gen 1:5).[13]

While I appreciate the LDS view that the Garden of Eden is in the Terrestrial realm and thus is perfect and unchanged versus the Telestial realm which fallen mankind now inhabits, I believe that the existence of Adam in the Garden of Eden and God's command to work the ground in the Garden of Eden would have caused changes so that nothing would have remained as created in this sense. Adam was given plants and fruit to eat in the Garden of Eden so this implies change and that death, at least for plants, was a change from the initial condition of creation.

The Nephites build a temple "after the manner of the temple of Solomon." However, this temple was not built "of so many precious things; for they were not to be found upon the land" (2 Ne 5:16–17). This statement appears contrary to 2 Ne 5:15 where Nephi teaches his people to build buildings "of wood, and or iron, and of steel, and of gold, and of silver, and of precious ores which were in great abundance."

Nephi predicts that the Messiah will be named Jesus Christ, the Son of God. (2 Ne 25:19). He also predicts that the Jews will crucify him and, after three days in a sepulcher, he will rise from the dead. (2 Ne 25:13). These prophecies are extremely detailed and precise compared to Old Testament prophets which points to either superior revelation or the author wrote these things from a historical perspective after these events occurred.[14]

In 2 Nephi 25:20, Nephi says, "there is none other name

---

13   Adam and Eve were thrust out of the Garden of Eden (Terrestrial) into the mortal sphere we now inhabit (Telestial). God, on the other hand, lives a Celestial existence even much greater than the Garden of Eden. The change was not wrought by Adam, but by God.

14   Again, a result of Joseph Smith's 1820s English Translation. Furthermore, as a prophet, Nephi was privy to revelation from God. Therefore, God could have told Nephi what he wished according to his will.

given under heaven save it be this Jesus Christ, of which I have spoken, whereby man can be saved." This statement appears to be a paraphrase of what the apostle Peter said to the Sanhedrin shortly after Pentecost (Acts 4:12). This is remarkable given that Peter was not familiar with Nephi's words. The other possible explanation is that the author of 2 Nephi lived after Peter and was familiar with his words.

Nephi refers to the Bible in 2 Nephi 29:3 and says that many Gentiles will reject the *Book of Mormon* because they already have a Bible and need nothing more. This prophecy is astounding because the term "Bible" was completely unknown in 600 BC when Nephi referred to it. The word "Bible" comes from the Greek word *biblia* for books or scrolls. Not all of the books of the Bible were written until 700 years later. Therefore, Nephi is referring to a collection of writings that only partially existed in his day and were not called the Bible. It is also noteworthy that Nephi predicts that the Gentiles would revere a collection of Jewish writings called the Bible while rejecting later Jewish writings called the *Book of Mormon*. It is difficult to accept this kind of predictive detail and precision unless the author of 2 Nephi wrote after the Bible existed.[15]

Nephi refers to "the gospel of Jesus Christ" (2 Ne 30:5). Nephi again uses words and defines concepts that were unknown until 630 years later. Nephi claims to prophesy but speaks in the past tense about the life of Christ in 2 Nephi 31:5–10. Nephi says that when Jesus was baptized with water, the Holy Spirit descended upon him in the form of a dove.

---

15 It is sad to many Mormons that mainstream Christians are often quick to dismiss The Book of Mormon as irrelevant—or worse—as whole cloth in light of its claim as a second witness to the same Champion of the Bible (Jesus Christ) they adore. One would think they would take more interest in at least reviewing its contents before so quickly casting away such a unique opportunity. One would think they would gladly embrace an additional witness that strengthens the message of the Bible.

THE BOOK OF JACOB

Fifty-five years after Lehi leaves Jerusalem, Nephi commands his brother Jacob to write preachings and revelations for the sake of their people. Nephi anoints a man to be king over the Nephites and then dies. The Nephites "grow hard in their hearts" and "indulge in wicked practices" such as desiring many wives and concubines (Jacob 1:15). Jacob tells them to follow the commands of God and not to seek after the riches of this world. He tells them to clothe the naked, feed the hungry, help the sick, and liberate the captive. Jacob commands them to have only one wife and no concubines. He says that the land will be cursed by God if they do not obey him.

Jacob says that the Lamanites are more righteous than the Nephites for they "have not forgotten the commandments of the Lord" (Jacob 3:5). Because the Lamanites have kept God's command to have only one wife, God will not destroy them but will make them a blessed people. Jacob commands the Nephites to no longer revile the Lamanites because of the darkness of their skin. He writes on plates to show that the knowledge of Christ and his glory were known hundreds of years before his coming. He says that the trees, mountains, and waves respond to his commands given "in the name of Jesus" (Jacob 4:6).

Jacob urges the Nephites to be reconciled to God through "the atonement of Christ, his Only Begotten Son" (Jacob 4:11). He quotes the prophet Zenos regarding the analogy of the tame and wild olive trees. The tame olive tree is the house of Israel that does not bear good fruit so its branches are cut off. Wild branches are grafted into the tame tree and bear good fruit. Eventually, the wild branches corrupt the tame tree roots so that only bad fruit is produced. The owner of the vineyard is grieved that the trees are corrupt and are only fit to be cut down and burned. The owner of the vineyard orders his servants to nourish the natural trees and remove the bad ones. The good fruit of the natural trees will be kept but that which is bad will be burned.

Jacob explains "those who labor diligently in the Lord's vineyard will be blessed while those who do not will be cursed. The world will be burned with fire. Those of the House of Israel who harden their hearts will die and be cast into the lake of fire and brimstone. Jacob urges his brethren to repent and enter "the strait gate and continue in the way which is narrow, until ye shall obtain eternal life" (Jacob 6:11).

A man named Sherem tells the Nephites that there is no Christ. He leads many away and confronts Jacob. Sherem says that Jacob has perverted the right way, which is to follow the laws of Moses. Sherem debates Jacob and asks Jacob for a sign to validate his teachings. Jacob says that God will smite Sherem, which causes him to fall down for many days. As Sherem nears death, he asks that the Nephites be gathered around him. He tells the Nephites that he was wrong to deny Christ and that he had been deceived by the devil. Sherem dies and the people return to God.

The Lamanites hate the Nephites and seek to destroy them by wars despite efforts by the Nephites to make peace. Jacob grows old and tells his son Enos to take his place. Enos promises to keep the commands of Nephi.

AUTHOR COMMENTS

As Nephi nears death, he anoints another man king. Jacob says that the people loved Nephi so much that all of their kings were called Nephi starting with second Nephi, third Nephi and so forth "according to the reigns of the kings" (Jacob 1:11). Jacob says that this practice continued through the reigns of all of the Nephite kings despite what the kings chose to call themselves. The perspective of this statement seems to be historic rather than prophetic. In addition, kings are absolute rulers and so it is highly unlikely that they would not be able to be called by their own names especially after all those who knew Nephi personally were dead. Finally, this prophecy does not appear to be accurate as subsequent Nephite kings such as King Benjamin and Mosiah were called by their own names.

Jacob quotes the prophet Zenos who tells a story about the House of Israel being like a tame olive tree in a vineyard.[16] The footnotes to this story in the *Book of Mormon* reference the analogy of the wild olive tree in Romans 11:13-24. Both stories are very similar which is remarkable since neither Paul nor Zenos had any knowledge of each other. This again begs the question of whether the author of The Book of Jacob wrote it after Romans was written.

The practice of men having multiple wives is condemned as wicked and abominable to God. Jacob says that the Lord commands that each man have one wife. Although the Lamanites are cursed by God for not following his commands, Jacob says that they do follow this one command. Because they do, Jacob says that God will not destroy them and that they will become a blessed people. This commandment appears to conflict with the polygamous practices of some Mormons.[17]

---

16 Zenos is not known as a prophet in the Bible for this is one of the "plain and precious things" that was lost and has been restored by the Mormon scriptures.

17 No mainstream Mormon practices polygamy without facing eventual excommunication. The only "Mormons" practicing polygamy since 1890 have been members of splinter groups that choose to refer to themselves as Mormons. Actually, this is consistent with what appears to man to be God's arbitrary stand on polygamy based on time and place. Usually, God forbids polygamy (As in Jacob's time, New Testament times, and contemporary times). However, in Abraham's time and David and Solomon's time and the early days of the restored

I believe Jesus dealt decisively with the subject of polygamy when he declared that it never was God's will but was the result of the sinful desires of man (Mt 19:4-9).

In Jacob 6:11, he says that eternal life is obtained by repentance, entering the strait gate and continuing in the narrow way. As previously seen in 2 Nephi, this teaching appears to be a process that leads to eternal life through good works. This contradicts many Bible verses and some verses in 2 Nephi that say eternal life is a gift given by God based on faith in Jesus Christ. (2 Ne 2:4–9 and 10:24; Titus 3:5; Gal 2:15 and 3:3; Philip 3:9)

church, it was sanctioned for a period of time. This demonstrates the need for continuing revelation through a *living prophet*.

THE BOOKS OF ENOS, JAROM, OMNI, AND THE WORDS OF MORMON

Enos is moved by the example of his father Jacob and prays to God to forgive his sins. Because of his faith in Christ, God removes his sins. Enos prays to God that a record of the Nephites will be preserved. God sees his faith and grants his request. The Nephites try to restore the Lamanites to true faith in God but they are unsuccessful. The Lamanites seek to destroy the Nephites. They are a bloodthirsty and filthy people.

The Nephites grow crops and raise cattle, goats, and horses. Enos diligently strives with the Nephites to teach them the fear of the Lord so they do not go down the path to destruction. Wars continue between the Lamanites and the Nephites throughout the life of Enos.

Jarom receives the plates from his father Enos. He says that some of the Nephites have hardened their hearts against God but there are also many who "have communion with the Holy Spirit" and have faith (Jarom 1:4). The Nephites withstand numerous attacks by the Lamanites and drive them from their land. The Nephites prosper but are warned to keep God's commands or they will be destroyed. When Jarom is old, he gives the plates to his son Omni.

Omni passes the plates to his son Amaron. The Nephites who do not follow God's commands are destroyed. Amaron delivers the plates to his brother Chemish who passes them to his son

Abinadom. Wars continue between the Lamanites and Nephites. Abinadom passes the plates to his son Amaleki.

The Nephite King Mosiah is told by God to flee into the wilderness. He flees to a land called Zarahemla. The people of this land rejoice when they meet the Nephites for they are descended from the Jews who fled Jerusalem when King Zedekiah was taken to Babylon. These Jews are descendants of a third emigration to the Americas that happened eleven years after the Nephites and included Mulek, the youngest son of King Zedekiah. King Mosiah dies and his son Benjamin becomes king. Amaleki gives the plates to King Benjamin. False Christs, prophets, and preachers continue among the Nephites after the time of King Benjamin, as do wars with the Lamanites.

The plates are handed down many generations until they come to a man named Mormon. Mormon lived hundreds of years after the coming of Christ to the Nephites. Mormon sees the destruction of the Nephites. [18]

AUTHOR COMMENTS

Enos lived hundreds of years before Christ, yet he says that his father taught him "in the nuture and admonition of the Lord" (Enos 1:1). This same phrase and idea is used by the apostle Paul in Ephesians 6:4. This phrase is not used anywhere else in the Bible and so is another example of either remarkable coincidence, unprecedented revelation or the author of Enos was familiar with the writings of Paul to the Ephesians. [19]

God forgives the sins of Enos based on his fervent prayers

---

18   It is important to note that the words of Mormon are commensurate with an editorial note by the abridger and namesake of *the Book of Mormon*. This explains why it is out of place chronologically. Its purpose is to provide a textual transition from the small plates to Mormon's abridgement of the large plates

19   Old Testament era folks were trained to look forward to and worship the coming of Christ. There is nothing unusual about this.

of faith. Enos asks God how this happened and God tells him "thy faith hath made thee whole" (Enos 1:8). This verse says that salvation is based on faith alone which agrees and conflicts with other verses in 2 Nephi and Jacob as previously discussed.

According to Jacob 1:10–11, the kings of the Nephites were named after Nephi in numerical order, despite what these kings called themselves. However, Omni refers to the Nephite King Mosiah and his son King Benjamin, which appears to contradict what the Book of Jacob says.

Amaleki pleads with the Nephites to believe in Christ, the Holy One of Israel "and partake of his salvation, and the power of his redemption." He continues by saying that they need to offer themselves totally to Christ, "continue in fasting and praying, and endure to the end; and as the Lord liveth ye will be saved" (Omni 1:26). This is another example of faith and endurance in good works to attain eternal life that conflicts with other verses in the *Book of Mormon* and the Bible that say eternal life is through faith in Jesus Christ alone.

For most Christians, the concept of eternal life means living with God in heaven. For LDS, it is more complicated in that almost everyone (except for a few sons of perdition), will wind up in one of three heavenly kingdoms: Celestial, Terrestrial, and Telestial. The vast majority of mankind will be glorified with resurrected bodies and live in much better places than this life. Therefore, good works for LDS members are related to spiritual development to god status (becoming like Jesus) and attaining a higher level in the Celestial Kingdom.

THE BOOK OF MOSIAH

King Benjamin teaches his sons to read the plates that are written in the language of the Egyptians. He instructs them in the commandments of God and the history of the Nephites. King Benjamin names his son Mosiah to succeed him. Mosiah gathers the people at the temple where King Benjamin tells them that they will prosper if they obey the Lord's commandments. He declares his son Mosiah to be the king and warns them not to rebel against God. Those who do not repent of their sins will be enemies of God and suffer eternal torment. Those who keep the commandments of God are blessed "both temporal and spiritual" and will dwell with God if they are faithful to the end (Mosiah 2:41).

King Benjamin tells the people the Lord God shall come from heaven and dwell with men. He will perform many miracles and suffer such anguish because of the wickedness of his people that "blood will flow from every pore (of his body)" (Mosiah 3:7). He will be called Jesus Christ the Son of God and his mother will be called Mary. Salvation shall come through faith in his name. He will be crucified and rise from the dead after three days. His blood will make atonement for "the sins of those who have fallen by the transgression of Adam, who have died not knowing the will of God concerning them or who have ignorantly died" (Mosiah 3:11). However, those who knowingly rebel against God can only be saved through repentance and faith in Jesus Christ.

The blood of Christ makes atonement for the sins of infants and little children. The people cry to God to have mercy on them through the atoning blood of Jesus. The Spirit of God comes upon them and they are filled with joy.

King Benjamin says that salvation comes to those who put their trust in the Lord, are diligent in keeping his commandments, and continue in the faith until death. He tells them to feed the hungry and care for the sick and poor. He warns them that they will perish if they do not keep the commandments of God and continue in their faith in Jesus Christ. The people respond by wishing to enter into a covenant with God to do his will and obey his commandments. King Benjamin says that they shall be called children of Christ because "this day he hath spiritually begotten you; for ye say that your hearts are changed through faith in his name; therefore, ye are born of him and have become his sons and daughters" (Mosiah 5:7). He tells them that they must beware lest their transgressions cause the name of Christ written on their hearts to be blotted out and they become numbered with the lost on the left hand of God. Therefore, he urges them to remain steadfast in faith and abound in good works so that Christ "may seal you his, that you may be brought to heaven, that ye may have everlasting salvation and eternal life" (Mosiah 5:15).

Mosiah succeeds Benjamin as king and walks in the ways of the Lord. King Mosiah sends Ammon and some strong men to the land of Lehi-Nephi. Ammon is brought before King Limhi who rejoices when he discovers that Ammon is from Zarahemla. King Limhi tells Ammon that his people are in bondage to the Lamanites. He also asks Ammon if he can translate twenty-four plates that some of his people found in the wilderness. Ammon can't translate them, but he tells the king that there is a seer among his people who can.

There follows an account of Zeniff, who leads people from Zarahemla to the land of Lehi-Nephi. Zeniff and his people are welcomed by King Laman who is a Lamanite and ruler of the land of Lehi-Nephi. They settle in the land but thirteen years later King Laman stirs his people against those of Zeniff. The people of Zeniff defeat the Lamanites and there is peace for twenty-two years. King Laman dies and his son stirs up the Lamanites against the people of Zeniff but they are again defeated. Zeniff confers his kingdom upon his son Noah who does not follow the commandments of God. He has many wives and concubines and he imposes heavy taxes upon the people. King Noah builds a palace and many fine buildings.

A man called Abinadi prophesies that the people of King Noah will be delivered into the hands of their enemies if they do not repent and turn from their wicked ways. He says that God will smite them with famine, pestilence, hail, and insects. The people become angry with Abinadi and bring him before King Noah who puts him in prison. Abinadi reviews the Ten Commandments and the Mosaic prophesies of Isaiah with the king and his priests. He tells them that God the Son will dwell among men and he will redeem his people. He will do many miracles before he is crucified. He will rise from the dead and ascend into heaven.

Abinadi says that those who believe the prophets and that the Lord will redeem his people are "heirs of the kingdom of God" (Mosiah 15:11-12). Those who are redeemed by Christ will partake of the first resurrection and dwell with God. Little children also shall have eternal life. The salvation of the Lord shall be declared to every nation, kindred, and people. A time will come when all shall see the salvation of the Lord and everyone shall confess that his judgments are just. The wicked shall be cast out and they shall howl, wail, weep, and gnash their teeth. Christ is the light and life of the world. Abinadi is burned to death for pronouncing God's judgments upon King Noah and his people.

The prophet Alma begins to teach the words of Abinadi concerning the death and resurrection of Christ. He teaches at a place called Mormon and baptizes two hundred and four followers. They are called The Church of Christ. Alma ordains priests and commands his followers to observe the Sabbath. King Noah sends troops to Mormon but Alma and his followers flee into the wilderness before they arrive.

Some of the king's people rebel and a man named Gideon fights with King Noah. While they are fighting, the Lamanites attack and Gideon spares the king. King Noah orders his people to flee because the Lamanites are too many to resist. Some of the people refuse to flee and plead for mercy from the Lamanites. The Lamanites allow those who surrender to return to their lands but they impose heavy taxes upon them. King Noah is killed by the men that fled into the wilderness with him because the king refused to let them return to their families. King Noah's son Limhi succeeds him. King Limhi and his people are guarded by the Lamanites and are forced to pay them one-half of their possessions.

The priests of King Noah continue to live in the wilderness after his death. They see some daughters of the Lamanites singing and dancing. The priests of Noah abduct some of the daughters and carry them into the wilderness. The Lamanites blame King Limhi and send their army to destroy them. The Lamanites are defeated and their king is captured and brought before King Limhi. When King Limhi learns that the Lamanites invaded because of the abduction of their daughters, he orders a search among his people. Gideon tells King Limhi that the priests of Noah are responsible. Peace is restored when the two kings realize what happened.

After many days, the Lamanites start to insult and mistreat the Nephites but they do not kill them because their king made peace with King Limhi. The people of Limhi complain to their king such that he decides to attack the Lamanites. However, they are defeated repeatedly by the Lamanites such that many of their men are killed and there are more women than men.

When Ammon and some of his men enter the city of King Limhi, they are arrested because they are mistaken for some of the priests of Noah. King Limhi rejoices when he discovers that Ammon and his men are from Zarahemla. King Limhi and Ammon decide to flee from the Lamanites and return to Zarahemla. They provide the Lamanites with wine and escape while they are in a drunken stupor. The Lamanites pursue them but do not find them in the wilderness. The people of Limhi arrive safely in Zarahemla and become the subjects of King Mosiah.

Alma is warned by the Lord to gather his people and flee into the wilderness because the soldiers of King Noah are approaching. They find a very beautiful and pleasant land where they settle and prosper. The people wish to make Alma their king but he refuses. He tells them to treat each other as equals and reminds them of the evil practices of King Noah. In this way, he persuades them not to have any kings. Alma consents to be their high priest. They build a city named Helam and multiply greatly in numbers. They are discovered by the Lamanites and become their servants. The Lamanites also find the priests of Noah in the wilderness and they also become their servants. One of the priests of Noah called Amulon is made king over the people of Alma by Laman who is the king of the Lamanites.

King Laman makes the priests of Noah teachers throughout his lands so the Lamanites learn the language of the Nephites. Amulon begins to persecute the people of Alma by giving them difficult tasks. The people respond by crying out to God until Amulon orders that anyone doing this will be put to death. God hears their cries and delivers them from bondage. God causes a deep sleep to come upon the Lamanites, which allows the people of Alma to escape to the land of Zarahemla.

King Mosiah gathers his people and reads them the accounts of the journeys of the people of Zeniff and Alma. The people give thanks and praise to God for delivering them from the Lamanites. Alma addresses them and says that they should remember that the Lord delivered them. King Limhi and many others are baptized by Alma and are added to the Church of God. Alma ordains many priests and establishes churches throughout the land. The priests are only allowed to preach what Alma tells them.

Many of the young generation reject the traditions and beliefs of their parents concerning Christ. They refuse to be baptized and join the church. There are dissensions among the church members. Some members are brought before Alma for many different kinds of inequities so that he can judge what should be done. God tells Alma he will freely forgive those who are baptized unto repentance and are received into the church. God also tells him that whoever confesses his sins "before thee and me, and repent in the sincerity of his heart, him shall ye forgive, and I will forgive him also" (Mosiah 26:29). Those who refuse to repent and confess their sins to Alma are not numbered among the people of the church and their names are blotted out.

The unbelievers persecute church members such that their leaders complain to Alma and King Mosiah. The king issues a proclamation to forbid the persecution of those who belong to the church of God. The sons of Mosiah are unbelievers as well as a son of Alma named Alma. Alma's son is a very wicked and an idolatrous man, who causes many dissensions among the people. He conspires with the sons of Mosiah to destroy the church. An angel of the Lord appears to them and tells them to stop persecuting the church. Alma is struck dumb and becomes so weak that he can't move. He is taken to his father where a crowd gathers to witness what God has done. Alma and his priests fast and pray that his son might be restored. After two days, he is healed and says that he has repented of his sins and is "born of the Spirit" (Mosiah 27:24). Alma's son and King Mosiah's sons travel throughout the land preaching the word of God and telling others what God has done for them.

The sons of Mosiah go to the Lamanites and declare the salvation of the Lord. They hope that the hatred of the Lamanites towards them will change once they come "to the knowledge of the Lord their God" (Mosiah 28:2). King Mosiah gathers the plates and translates them by using the Urim and Thummim stones. The translated records include a history of events from the creation of Adam. King Mosiah gives the plates and translations to the son of Alma.

King Mosiah asks his people who should succeed him. The people want his son Aaron but he and his brothers refuse to be king and they go to the land of Nephi to preach to the Lamanites. King Mosiah decides to remain king until his death and tells his people that there will be no more kings after him. He appoints judges so that the people might be "judged of God rather than of man." He says that "because all men are not just it is not expedient that ye should have a king or kings rules over you" (Mosiah 29:16). The people select judges to decide matters related to their laws. The son of Alma is appointed the first chief judge as well as their high priest. The son of Alma judges according to the ways of the Lord. Alma and King Mosiah die.

AUTHOR COMMENTS

King Benjamin addresses his people and tells them that those who do not keep the commandments of God and do not repent but remain enemies to God will be doomed to never-ending torment. (Mosiah 2:37-39). "Those that keep the commandments of God...are blessed in all things, both temporal and spiritual; and if they hold out faithful to the end they are received into heaven, that thereby they may dwell with God in a state of everlasting happiness" (Mosiah 2:41). This passage teaches that prosperity can be achieved by obeying the commandments of God. This teaching is seen in the Palestine covenant of the Bible where God promises prosperity to the Israelites if they keep his commandments (Deut 30:9-10).

King Benjamin also says that salvation is promised by God to those who both keep the commandments and remain faithful to the end. The Bible teaches that mankind can't keep the commandments of God and therefore heaven can't be attained by obedience (Rom 3:20). Therefore, nobody can be declared righteous based on observing the laws of God (Gal 2:15). Rather it is by faith in Jesus Christ that we are forgiven and can dwell with God in heaven. (Eph 2:8-9; Phillip 3:8-9). The purpose of God's commandments are to make us aware of our sins and our need to be forgiven through the blood of Jesus (Heb 7:27). The crucifixion of Jesus paid the penalty of death for all who believe and so satisfies the requirement for failing to keep God's commandments (Rom 6:23; 10:4).

King Benjamin says that an angel from God told him that the Messiah would be called Jesus Christ the Son of God. His mother shall be named Mary. None of the Old Testament prophets of the Bible were able to provide the name of the Messiah and his mother so either this is a superior revelation or it was written after the fact. He also says that Jesus will be crucified and rise from the dead after three days so that "salvation might come unto the children of men even through faith on his name" (Mosiah 3:9). This statement that faith alone is required for salvation contradicts King Benjamin's previous one recorded in Mosiah 2:41.

King Benjamin tells his people that the blood of Jesus "atoneth for the sins of those who have fallen by the transgressions of Adam, who have died not knowing the will of God concerning them, or who have ignorantly sinned" (Mosiah 3:11). Since all men have fallen by the sin of Adam, this means that most people will go to heaven since they do not know God's commandments, which are based on the books of the Bible. Indeed the only people that go to hell are those who know but transgress the commands of God. This teaching conflicts with what Jesus said that most people will perish and relatively few will be saved (Matt 7:13–14). It also appears to conflict with D&C 132:5 which says that "broad is the gate, and wide the way that leadeth to the deaths; and many there are that go in there at." The use of the word "deaths" presumably refers to the LDS belief that some will suffer in hell for a season (first death) before being exalted to the Telestial kingdom. The plural use of the word death implies that most people will experience the second or permanent death of remaining in hell. This contradicts the LDS belief that most people will reside in one of three heavenly kingdoms and only a few sons of perdition will ultimately remain in hell. In addition, this teaching of King Benjamin leads to perverse results in that LDS missionaries are actually bringing the possibility of damnation to people who would otherwise be ignorant of God's commandments. Mosiah 3:20–22 says that people will not be judged blameless (except for little children) after the knowledge of the Savior has been taught "throughout every nation, kindred, tongue, and people." Mosiah 4:6–7 says that faith in the Lord plus keeping his commandments and remaining "in the faith unto death" will result in salvation. This is a faith plus works plus perseverance in being good formula that contradicts the Bible. This formula is repeated in Mosiah 4:30 and 5:7–8 and is based on human effort rather than the grace and mercy of God. There are verses in Mosiah that clearly state that salvation is not possible except through repentance and faith in Jesus Christ (Mosiah 3:12, 17).

I have been told by an LDS reviewer that there is an explanation for these seemingly contradictory verses. The LDS view agrees that it is through faith in the atonement of Jesus that all mankind (except for the sons of perdition) are saved and resurrected into one of three heavenly kingdoms. However, it is through keeping the commandments of God that some are perfected becoming like God and dwelling with him in the highest or Celestial heaven.[20] Therefore, the LDS concept of salvation is more complex and explains the emphasis on works in salvation.

Alma becomes high priest and baptizes those who believe his teachings. With the approval of King Mosiah, he ordains priests and establishes churches among the Nephites. The priests are only allowed to preach the words of Alma. God speaks to Alma and tells him that those who sincerely confess their sins and are forgiven by Alma will also be forgiven by God (Mosiah 26:29). Furthermore, those would not repent and confess their sins were not numbered among the church and had their names blotted out

---

20   Mormon reviewer personal communication

(Mosiah 26:36). The footnote to this verse in the *Book of Mormon* references The Book of Life. This appears to say these people were not only thrown out of the church but were counted among those sons of perdition whose fate is hell.

The power to forgive sins invested in Alma does not appear to be consistent with the atonement of sins through faith in Jesus. Presumably, believers who are church members would be coming to Alma to confess their sins. This appears to interject the idea that salvation (in the sense of a heaven or hell issue) come through the grace of God administered through priests much as the Roman Catholics believe.

The forgiveness of sins by the head of the churches adds another layer of complexity to the faith only, plus keeping the commandments and being good unto death salvation messages found in this book. In contrast, the Bible teaches that all those who believe in Jesus as their savior and confess him as their Lord shall have everlasting life (John 1:12–13; 3:16–18; Rom 10:9–10).

THE BOOK OF ALMA

Following the death of King Mosiah, Alma becomes judge and is challenged by a man called Nehor. Nehor goes among the people teaching that the priests should not labor but should be supported by the people. He also teaches that all men will be saved. Gideon opposes Nehor and is killed by him. Alma judges that Nehor must die. Nehor confesses that his teachings are in error prior to his death. Those who do not belong to the church begin to persecute those who do. Some church members leave the church. Those who remain prosper and are generous to those in need.

A man named Amlici becomes popular among the Nephites who are not among the people of the church. Amlici is a wicked man determined to destroy the church. His supporters want to make him king but he is rejected by the majority of the people. His supporters make him king anyway and war results. Alma leads the Nephites against the followers of Amlici and defeats them. Amlici flees to the Lamanites who join with him and return to fight Alma and the Nephites. The Nephites defeat the Lamanites and Alma kills Amlici.

The remaining Nephites under Alma rededicate themselves to the church and many of them are baptized. The Nephites prosper but some begin to "wax proud" wearing rich apparel and setting their hearts on "the vain things of the world"(Alma 4:8). The proud church people begin to act scornfully towards those who do not act and believe the same. They also turn away from those in need. Alma appoints Nephihah to be chief judge so that he can devote himself to preaching the word of God among the people but he continues to act as high priest.

Alma teaches the people about their history. He tells them that they must put their trust in God, have a changed heart (be born again), do good works and remain faithful to death. He says that Jesus Christ will come and "take away the sins of the world, yea, the sins of every man who steadfastly believe on his name" (Alma 5:48). He calls on them "to repent and be born again" (Alma 5:49). Alma ordains priests and elders by laying his hands upon them. Those who do not belong to the church have their names blotted out of the book of life.

Alma teaches that Jesus will be born of the Virgin Mary "at Jerusalem which is the land of our forefathers" (Alma 7:10). Jesus will "take upon him death, that he may lose the bonds of death that bind his people" (Alma 7:12). He tells them to "repent and be born again; for the Spirit saith that if ye are not born again ye cannot inherit the kingdom of heaven; therefore, come and be baptized unto repentance that ye may be washed from your sins, that ye may have faith in the Lamb of God, who taketh away the sins of the world, who is mighty to save and to cleanse from all unrighteousness" (Alma 7:14). Alma says that those who are baptized to show their repentance and enter into a covenant with God to keep his commandments henceforth shall have eternal life. He stirs up the people to awaken them to their sense of duty so that they might abound in doing good works.

Alma travels to the land of Ammonihah and preaches but he is rejected. An angel of the Lord appears to Alma and tells him to continue to preach to the people of Ammonihah. He is told that they will be destroyed if they do not repent. Alma meets a man named Amulek who joins him in preaching to the people of Ammonihah. God gives them power such that they can't be confined in prison or killed. Alma tells them to repent and return to the ways of God or they will be destroyed. The people respond by arguing and getting angry with Alma such that they want to put him in prison.

Amulek addresses the people and says that he was like them until an angel appeared to him and told him that Alma is a holy man. The people remain skeptical and have lawyers question them. Amulek reads the minds of the lawyers and tells the people that their perverse lawyers and judges are the foundation of their destruction. A lawyer named Zeezrom tells Amulek that he will give him gold if he denies God. Amulek refuses and says that the Son of God is "the very Eternal Father" (Alma 11:39). He says that the Son of God will "take upon him the transgressions of those who believe in his name; and those are they that shall have eternal life, and salvation cometh to none else" (Alma 11:40).

Zeezrom begins to tremble "under a consciousness of his guilt" (Alma 12:1). Alma tells Zeezrom about the judgment and everlasting torments for those who do not heed the revelations of God. Zeezrom begins to ask questions so that he might know more concerning the kingdom of God. Alma tells him that those who reject God's words will experience a second or spiritual death and be tormented in the lake of fire. He says that all mankind is lost and fallen because of the sin of Adam in partaking of the forbidden fruit. However, those who repent and do not harden their hearts will receive mercy through God's Only Begotten Son and enter God's rest. Many of the people believe Alma's words. They repent and begin to study the scriptures. However, most of the people want to kill Alma and Amulek. Alma and Amulek are bound and brought before the chief judge. Zeezrom pleads for them and is reviled by the people. The people gather those who believe the words of Alma and Amulek and burn them.

Alma and Amulek are cast into prison where they are beaten and questioned. The chief judge and other leaders of Ammonihah gather in the prison. They mock Alma and Amulek saying that they will believe if them if they can break their bonds. Alma prays to God and their bonds are broken. The earth shakes such that the prison collapses falling on the chief judge and the leaders. Alma and Amulek are not harmed. They walk out of the rubble of the prison. The people flee when they see that their leaders are dead but Alma and Amulek are alive.

Alma and Amulek go to the City of Sidon where they find Zeezrom and others who believe their words. Zeezrom is sick with a fever caused by his fear that Alma and Amulek are dead because of his sins. Alma prays for Zeezrom who is immediately healed. Zeezrom is baptized and begins to preach to the people. Alma establishes a church and selects priests and teachers.

The Lamanites invade the land of Zarahemla and destroy the City of Ammonihah. Zoram leads the Nephites in pursuit of the Lamanites. He defeats them and frees those that were taken captive. However, all the rest of the people of Ammonihah are destroyed.

Alma encounters the sons of Mosiah while traveling to the land of Manti. He rejoices and learns that the sons of Mosiah have been successful in bringing many to the knowledge of the truth among the Lamanites. Ammon tells of how he separated from his brothers after entering the land of the Lamanites. He goes to the land of Ishmael where he is bound and taken to King Lamoni. Ammon finds favor with the king and becomes his servant tending his flocks. Some Lamanites scatter the king's flocks at a watering place named Sebus. Ammon confronts the troublemakers and kills seven of them with his sling and sword.

King Lamoni is surprised and curious about the source of Ammon's strength. Ammon tells him about God, the history of their people and Jesus Christ. The king believes him and falls down as if dead for two days. The queen calls for Ammon who tells her that the king is not dead but asleep. The queen believes him and is present when the king awakes at the time predicted by Ammon. The Spirit of God is poured out upon the king, queen and servants present such that they all fall down as though dead. Others gather to see what is happening including the brother of one of the men killed by Ammon at Sebus. This brother draws his sword and tries to kill Ammon but falls dead before striking him. God revives them and they begin to teach their people the words of Ammon. Those who believe establish a church among the Lamanites.

The Lord directs Ammon to go to Middoni to free his brothers who are in prison. King Lamoni goes with him to persuade King Antiomno who is his friend. They meet Lamoni's father who is king over all the Lamanites. His father becomes angry when he learns his son is helping a Nephite and orders Lamoni to kill Ammon. King Lamoni refuses so his father draws his sword to kill his son. Ammon intervenes so the old king tries to kill him. Ammon fights him and defeats him. The old king agrees to forgive his son and free Ammon's brothers in exchange for his life.

The brothers of Ammon are released from prison and go to the father of Lamoni. One of Ammon's brothers named Aaron tells the king about the scriptures, the plan of redemption and Jesus Christ. The king asks Aaron what he must do to have eternal life. Aaron replies that he must repent of his sins, call on the name of Jesus in faith, and believe in the atonement of Christ. The king does this and proclaims that Aaron, Ammon, and their brothers are free to preach the word of God among the Lamanites. Aaron and his brothers travel throughout the land of the Lamanites and establish churches. Those who believe become known as the Anti-Nephi-Lehi.

The remainder of the Lamanites who do not believe the words of God join with the Amalekites and the Amulonites to wage war on the Anti-Nephi-Lehis. The Anti-Nephi-Lehis refuse to fight and one thousand and five are slain without resistance. The Lamanites are convicted of their sin in killing their brothers. They stop attacking and are so impressed that more of them are converted than were killed. The Lamanites decide to attack the Nephites and destroy the people of Ammonihah.

The Amalekites begin to kill the Anti-Nephi-Lehis. Ammon gathers them and goes to the land of Zarahemla where they are received with joy. The Anti-Nephi-Lehis are given the land of Jershon and dwell with the Nephites.

A man named Korihor begins to preach in the land of Zarahemla that there is no Christ or atonement for sins. He says that there is no life after death. The Nephites bind him and take him to Alma the high priest. Korihor demands a sign from Alma to prove that what he says is true. Korihor is struck dumb whereupon he writes that he has been deceived by the devil that appeared to him as an angel of light. Korihor remains dumb because Alma says that he would continue to deceive others if his speech is restored. Korihor becomes a beggar and is killed.

The Zoramites pervert the ways of the Lord by worshipping idols. Alma goes to them and finds that they are a wicked and perverse people whose hearts are set on gold, silver, and fine goods. Alma and his brothers pray and go throughout the land preaching the word of God. They begin to have success among the poor who are not allowed into their synagogues because of the coarseness of their apparel. Amulek joins Alma in preaching to the people. He tells them that "according to the great plan of the Eternal God there must be an atonement made, or else all mankind must unavoidably perish" (Alma 34:9). He says that this atonement is possible only through the death of Jesus, which makes it an infinite and eternal sacrifice. Amulek exhorts them to pray continually to avoid being "led away by the temptations of the devil, that he may not overpower you, that ye may not become his subjects at the last day" (Alma 34:39). He teaches that men are possessed by the spirit of God or the devil. Whichever spirit is in possession at the death of each person determines his or her eternal destiny in heaven or hell.

The rulers and priests of the Zoramites cast out those who believe the words of God. Alma leads these believers to the land of Jershon. The Zoramites join with the Lamanites and attack the Nephites.

Alma gives his son Helaman the plates of brass and other scriptures. He also gives him the ball called Liahona which is the compass made by God. He says that it indicated the direction to the Promised Land and worked according to their faith in God. Alma praises his son Shiblon for his faithfulness to God despite suffering persecution. He tells him to "learn of me that there is no other way or means whereby man can be saved, only in and through Christ. Behold, he is the life and the light of the world. Behold, he is the word of truth and righteousness" (Alma 38:9). He tells him to be filled with love, to bridle his passions and refrain from idleness. Alma is critical of his son, Corianton, for leaving the ministry of the word and denying the Holy Ghost. He commands him to refrain from sin and return to the Lord.

Alma teaches his son that everyone will be resurrected from the dead. He says that "the spirits of all men, as soon as they are departed from this mortal body, yea, the spirits of all men, whether they be good or evil, are taken home to that God that gave them life" (Alma 40:11). Those who are righteous "are received to a state of happiness" while the wicked "are cast out into outer darkness" (Alma 40:12). The souls of all men remain thus until the time of their resurrection. All men shall be judged and rewarded according to their deeds. Alma tell his son to "see that you are merciful unto your brethren; deal justly, judge righteously, and do good continually; and if ye do all these things, then shall ye receive your reward; yea, ye shall have mercy restored to you again" (Alma 41:14).

Men are sinful due to transgressions of God's laws and must be redeemed. "God himself atoneth for the sins of the world, to bring about the plan of mercy, to approve the demands of justice that God might be a perfect, just God, and a merciful God also" (Alma 42:15). Alma exhorts his son to preach the word "that thou mayest bring souls unto repentance" (Alma 42:31).

The Ammonites are given lands among the Nephites and support their armies but do not fight the Lamanites. Moroni commands the Nephites armies and leads them to victory over the Lamanite army. Moroni demands that the Lamanites lay down their arms and swear never to take up arms against the Nephites.

The leader of the Lamanites, Zerahemmah, refuses these terms. The fighting resumes until Zerahemmah changes his mind when he sees that he and his men are being slaughtered by the Nephites who surround them.

Alma prophesies that the Nephites will be completely destroyed four hundred years after Jesus visits them. They will become extinct because of their unbelief and iniquities. Alma disappears while traveling to the land of Melek and is never seen again. The people believe that he was taken by God as nothing was ever found about his death and burial.

The Nephites grow rich and proud refusing to walk uprightly before God. Those who reject the words of Alma's son, Helaman, are led by a large and strong man named Amalickiah. Amalickiah persuades some of the Nephites to make him king. Moroni opposes Amalickiah and becomes the leader of the true believers in Jesus Christ called Christians. Moroni gathers those who are faithful to take up the cross against Amalickiah. Amalickiah flees to the Lamanites. Moroni requires that those who follow Amalickiah swear allegiance or die. A few followers choose death but most swear allegiance.

Amalickiah gains the favor of Lehonti, the Lamanite king, and becomes the commander of their army. One of his servants poisons Lehonti and Amalickiah becomes king. The servants of Amalickiah go to the king of the land of Nephi. One of the servants stabs the king in the heart while pretending to honor him. The Lamanites march on the Nephite city of Ammonihah but do not attack it because of the strong fortifications. They decide to go to the city of Noah and attack it but can't break its fortifications. Moroni drives the Lamanites out and the Nephites enjoy a time of peace and prosperity.

A land dispute arises among the Nephites living in the land of Morianton and Lehi. The people of Lehi appeal to Moroni for help whereupon the people of Morianton flee to the Lamanites. Moroni learns of their plans to flee and sends an army led by Teancum to intercept them. Teancum kills their leader, Morianton, and returns the people who followed him to their land where they are reconciled to the people of Lehi.

Pahoran succeeds his father Nephihah as chief judge and governor. Some of the people petition Pahoran to change a few points of their laws. Pahoran refuses and those who want the changes say that Pahoran should no longer be the chief judge. These people desire a king but they are opposed by those called free men. During this dispute, Amalickiah invades with his Lamanite army. The Nephites who want a king refuse to fight the Lamanites. Moroni is empowered by the governor to lead an army against the Nephites who refuse to fight. Four thousand of the dissenters called king men are killed and the rest are compelled to take up arms against the Lamanites. Amalickiah's army attacks and captures the city of Moroni as well as other cities. Teancum leads a Nephite army against Amalickiah. While the two armies are camped, Teancum enters the camp of Amalickiah at night and kills him while he is asleep.

Amalickiah's brother, Ammoron, succeeds him as king. Moroni joins Teancum and they devise a plan to draw the Lamanites out of the city of Mulek. Teancum marches past the city with a small force, which entices the Lamanites out of the city. Teancum flees and draws the Lamanites further away from their city. Moroni enters the city, which is lightly defended. He then pursues the Lamanites from behind. Teancum is reinforced by the army commanded by Lehi. When the Lamanites discover this, they flee back towards their city and encounter Moroni's army. The Lamanites are surrounded and are killed or taken prisoner.

The Lamanite prisoners are forced to fortify the city called Bountiful that is used to hold them. The Ammonites desire to take up arms and join the Nephites but Helaman persuades them not to do it. Helaman fears that the Ammonites would "lose their souls" because they previously made a covenant with God never to take up arms (Alma 53:15). However, the sons of the Ammonites who did not take this oath do take up arms. This is how two thousand young men came to serve under the command of Helaman.

Moroni and Ammoron exchange epistles demanding terms to end the fighting. The terms are mutually rejected. Moroni chooses a man called Laman and a small number of others to take wine to the Lamanites in the city of Gid. The Lamanites guarding the city get drunk and fall asleep. Moroni sneaks into the city and brings arms to the Nephite prisoners while the guards are sleeping. When the Lamanites wake up, they find themselves surrounded by Moroni's army and armed prisoners within the city. They surrender without fighting. The Lamanite prisoners are forced to fortify the city of Gid.

Helaman and the two thousand young Ammonites march past the Lamanite stronghold of Antiparah. The Lamanites come out to attack them but Helaman's army flees. Antipus leads a Nephite army in pursuit of the Lamanites. The Lamanites are trapped between the armies of Helaman and Antipus. A furious battle ensues and the Lamanites are defeated. Afterwards, it is discovered that none of the two thousand young Ammonites are killed in the battle.

Moroni sends an embassy to the governor of Zarahemla requesting troops and supplies. Only two thousand men and supplies are sent to Moroni who is besieging the city of Manti. The Lamanites in Manti learn that Moroni's army is much smaller than theirs is. They decide to come out and attack Moroni who flees and sends a small force to take the city. The Lamanites pursue Moroni's army deep into the wilderness. That night the Lamanites pitch their tents and expect that Moroni's army would do the same. However, Moroni commands his men to march around the Lamanites such that by morning they are inside the city of Manti. When the Lamanites discover this, they flee from the land.

Moroni sends an epistle to Pahoran, who is governor of Zarahemla, requesting reinforcements. The Lamanites attack and capture the city of Nephihah. Pahoran writes Moroni and explains that reinforcements have not been sent because of a rebellion among the Nephites. A man named Pachus has been appointed king over those who reject Pahoran. Pahoran flees to the land of

Gideon and asks Moroni to help him. Moroni takes a small force, which swells to thousands as he marches to the land of Gideon. Moroni joins with the army of Pahoran and they march to the city of Zarahemla. In the ensuing battle, Pachus is killed and his men are taken prisoner. Pahoran is restored to his judgment seat. Those who refuse to take up arms against the Lamanites are executed.

Moroni sends troops and supplies to reinforce Helaman's army and to fortify the land against the Lamanites. Moroni leads an army against the land of Nephihah. Moroni defeats the Lamanites and takes many prisoners. Many of the captured Lamanites join the people of Ammon and settle with them in peace. Moroni continues to pursue the Lamanites from city to city until they gather in the land of Moroni with their king Ammoron. While the armies are camped near each other, Teancum enters the Lamanite camp at night and kills Ammoron. However, Teancum is killed before he can escape. Moroni attacks the Lamanites the next morning and defeats them. Moroni completes the fortifications needed to defend against future Lamanite invasions. He returns to Zarahemla and yields command of his armies to his son Moronihah. Moroni retires to live the remainder of his days in peace. Helaman begins to preach the word of God. The church is re-established and the people prosper.

Shiblon takes possession of the sacred things delivered to Helaman by Alma. Moroni dies and a large company of Nephites under a man named Hagoth departs by ship. Many more Nephites also depart by ship and are never seen again.

AUTHOR COMMENTS

Alma preaches to the people of Nephi in the "church" in the city of Zarahemla. He tells them that they must be "born again" in order to have their names written in "the book of life" (Alma 5:49; 58). The date that this occurs is around 83 BC. All of these terms: "church," "born again," and "the book of life" are not mentioned in the Old Testament books of the Bible. A case can be made that the "book" mentioned in Exodus 32:33 could be "the book of life" but this term is not used. The term "church" is first used by Jesus in Matthew 16:18; "born again" is first used by Jesus in John 3:3 and "the book of life" is first mentioned in Revelation 20:12. These are further examples of either superior revelation compared to the Old Testament prophets or the author wrote the book of Alma after the New Testament books were written.

The editorial summary for Chapter 5 states that "To gain salvation, men must repent and keep the commandments, be born again, cleanse their garments through the blood of Christ, be humble and strip themselves from pride and envy, and do the works of righteousness." This summary says that salvation is based on faith in Jesus Christ plus good works. This message is consistent with some passages in Alma and other books such as Mosiah and Omni. However, many passages in Alma say that repentance and being born again through faith in Jesus Christ alone are sufficient for salvation. Refer to Table 1 for a comparison of some of the passages in Alma and some other books that illustrate the conflicting messages regarding what it takes to be saved and go to heaven after death.

Alma 5:48 says, "every man that steadfastly believeth in his (Jesus) name shall be saved." This statement implies that it is possible to be born again but loose salvation through a failure of faith afterwards. This verse supports the Armenian view that salvation is contingent upon continual personal effort through good works following a spiritual birth. Alma 53:14–15 says that Helaman feared that the Ammonites would "lose their souls" if they took up arms and thereby broke the covenant they had made with God. While repentance and faith in Jesus Christ is taught by Alma, there are conflicting verses regarding whether good works and personal diligence in keeping the faith are also necessary. Alma seems to say that he has the power to "grant an inheritance at my right hand" (Alma 5:58). This is in the context of his teaching about the separation of the righteous and the wicked. Thus, he seems to be saying that he has the power to appoint men to unto places in heaven "at his right hand." Similar power granted to Alma is evidenced in Mosiah 26: 29;36.

Table 1 Selected Salvation Verses

Citation	Quote	Salvation Requirements
Alma 5:12	And according to his faith, there was a mighty change wrought in his heart.	Alma saved by faith
Alma 5:13	...they humbled themselves and put their trust in the true and living God. And behold, they were faithful until the end; therefore they were saved.	Fathers of the people in the church in Zarahemla saved by repentance, faith and good works
Alma 5:14	...have ye spiritually been born of God? Have ye received his image in your countenances? Have ye experienced this mighty change in your hearts?	Alma questions the church members of Zarahemla regarding whether they have been born again through faith in Jesus Christ
Alma 5:21	...there can no man be saved except his garments are washed white; yea, his garments must be purified until they are cleansed from all stain, through the blood of him of whom it has been spoken by our fathers; who should come to redeem his people from their sins.	Alma tells the church members of Zarahemla that they can only be saved by the blood sacrifice of Jesus Christ in which there is forgiveness and redemption from their sins.
Alma 5:49 5:51	...I say unto you the aged, and also the middle aged, and the rising generation; yea, to cry unto them that they must repent and be born again. Repent, for except ye repent ye can in nowise inherit the kingdom of heaven.	Alma tells the church members of Zarahemla that they must see themselves as sinners, turn from their sins and experience a spiritual birth through faith in Jesus Christ to enter heaven.

Citation	Quote	Salvation Requirements
Alma 6:14–16	Now I say unto you that ye must repent, and be born again; for the Spirit saith if ye are not born again ye cannot inherit the kingdom of heaven; therefore come and be baptized unto repentance, they ye may be washed from your sins, that ye may have faith on the Lamb of God, who taketh away the sins of the world, who is mighty to save and to cleanse from all unrighteousness...and whosoever doeth this, and keepeth the commandments of God from thenceforth, the same...shall have eternal life...	Alma preaches to the people in the city of Gideon that they must repent of their sins, have faith in Jesus Christ and keep the commandments to have eternal life.
Alma 11:40	And he shall come into the world to redeem his people; and he shall take upon him the transgressions of those who believe on his name; and these are they that shall have eternal life; and salvation cometh to none else.	Amulek contends with Zeezrom and tells him that only those who believe in Jesus Christ shall be saved.
Alma 22:13–14	And Aaron did expound unto him the scriptures ...the plan of redemption that was prepared from the foundation of the world, through Christ, for all whosoever would believe on his name. And since man had fallen, he could not merit anything of himself; but the sufferings and death of Christ atone for their sins, through faith and repentance, and so forth...	Aaron preaches to King Lamoni's father that faith in Jesus Christ and not good works are the basis for forgiveness of sins.

Citation	Quote	Salvation Requirements
Alma 25:16	Now they did not suppose that salvation came by the law of Moses; but the law of Moses did serve to strengthen their faith in Christ; and thus they did retain a hope through faith, unto eternal salvation, relying upon the spirit of prophecy, which spake of those things to come.	The Lamanites who joined with the people of Anti-Nephi-Lehi kept the laws of Moses realizing that salvation did not come from this but through faith in Christ and the prophecies regarding him.
Alma 32:13	...whosoever repenteth shall find mercy; and he that findeth mercy and endureth to the end the same shall be saved.	Alma teaches the people on the hill Onidah that those who are humble and repent, believe and do good works to the end shall be saved
Alma 38:9	...ye may learn of me that there is no other way or means whereby man can be saved, only through Christ. Behold, he is the life and the light of the world. Behold, he is the word of truth and righteousness.	Alma instructs his son Shiblon that only through Jesus Christ is salvation possible.

As is evident from the preceding examples, there are many verses in Alma that state that it is necessary to be born again spiritually through faith in Jesus Christ in order to be saved and have eternal life in the kingdom of heaven. For example, Alma says that salvation only comes through faith in Jesus (Alma 11:40). The LDS view of salvation includes universal atonement for all mankind through the sacrifice of Jesus. Virtually everyone will be resurrected and live in one of three heavenly kingdoms. The only exceptions are the sons of perdition, those who reject Jesus and seek to serve Satan. The LDS concept of salvation has three parts: resurrection (which everyone will experience), attaining one of the three kingdoms, and exaltation by which some will become like God and dwell in the highest (Celestial) kingdom. The salvation by faith in Jesus statement here and many other places in the *Book of Mormon* do not make sense except for those who attain the Celestial kingdom since most people do not have faith in Jesus yet will be resurrected as glorious beings in the Terrestrial or Telestial kingdoms. The revelation of these three heavenly kingdoms was not given until 1832 to Joseph Smith (D&C 76). Therefore, those who heard this message must have thought that faith in Jesus is a heaven or hell issue. The LDS view is that this is not deception but represents the progressive revelation of truth.

Alma 7:10 says that a woman named Mary will be the mother of Jesus and that he will be born "at Jerusalem." According to the *Book of Mormon*, Alma said this around 83 BC. Naming Mary as the mother of Jesus is not found in the Old Testament books of the Bible and so this represents either superior revelation or this was written afterwards. The statement that Jesus would be born "at Jerusalem" conflicts with the Bible, which says that Jesus was born in Bethlehem (Luke 2:4; Matt 2:1). This apparent contradiction is explained by Mormons by viewing Bethlehem as in the land of Jerusalem since it is only five miles from Bethlehem. They point out that locals considered the city of Hebron that is twenty-five miles from Bethlehem to still be in the land of Jerusalem.

Zeezrom asks Amulek if the Son of God (i.e., Jesus) is the "very Eternal Father" to which he responds that Jesus "is the very Eternal Father of heaven and earth, and all things which in them are; he is the beginning and the end, the first and the last" (Alma 11:38–39). The footnote references in the *Book of Mormon* cite Isaiah 9:6 that refer to the child (Jesus) that was to be born and would be called "Wonderful Counselor, Mighty God, Everlasting Father, Prince of Peace." These verses seem to say that Jesus and the Father are one God in being. However, there is also a reference to Mosiah 15:2–4 in which Jesus is called the Son of God because he "subjected the flesh to the will of the Father, being the Father and the Son. The Father because he was conceived by the power of God; and the Son, because of the flesh; thus becoming the Father and Son." This is the clearest reference I have found to support the LDS view that Jesus and the Father are one in will but that Jesus is the first-born and pre-eminent spirit child created by the Father. However, verse four says, "they are one God, yea, the very Eternal Father of heaven and of earth." The eternality of the Father and the Son appears to conflict with the idea that the Father created the Son as a spirit child and then as a human being which is the view held by some who call themselves Mormons. The nature of God is a complex subject with differing views among Mormons and is discussed in greater detail in the Reflections Chapter.

Alma 21:4 refers to "synagogues" where people receive preaching. This occurs between 90 and 77 BC according to the *Book of Mormon*. The term synagogue refers to Jewish places of worship after the destruction of Solomon's temple in 586 BC. This was after the arrival of Lehi and his family in the Promised Land of the Americas in 590 BC so they could not have known this term.

Alma 34:34–35 says that either the Holy Spirit or an evil spirit possess every person's body. At the time of death, whichever spirit is in possession will "have the power to possess your body in that eternal world." Alma teaches and warns not to delay in repentance or the devil will seal you and the Lord "hath no place in you." This clearly infers that these people will be doomed to eternal destruction in hell. This appears to conflict with the LDS belief that some will hear and accept the gospel while in hell and be saved.[21]

Alma appears to teach the Armenian view that it is possible to lose salvation as he urges his brethren to "pray continually, that ye may not be led away by the temptations of the devil, that he may not overpower you, that ye may not become his subjects at the last day" (Alma 34:39). This also is reflected in D&C 20:32,

---

21 I think Mormons generally think that if a person has had a genuine and legitimate opportunity to accept the gospel and still refuses it, then yes, what you suggest is correct. But we're not in a position to make that judgment, which is up to God.

which says that it is possible for a person to depart from grace and God. However, this contradicts D&C 50:42, which says, "none of them that my Father hath given me shall be lost."[22]

The Holy Ghost is referred to as "it" in Alma 34:38. This conflicts with the Bible, which refers to the Holy Ghost as a person (John 14:16–17; 16:13).[23] Later Alma 43:14 says that the Lamanites were nearly as numerous as the Nephites. Alma 43:21 says that the Lamanites were much more numerous than the Nephites, which is an apparent contradiction.

A man named Korihor is deceived by the devil that appears to him as an angel of light. He preaches that there is no God until confronted by Alma. Korihor challenges Alma to show him a sign that there is a God. Alma obliges and Korihor immediately becomes dumb. Korihor then repents and writes that he "always knew there was a God" but that he was deceived by the devil. He pleads with Alma to restore his speech but Alma refuses saying that he would again lead the people away from God. This appears to be a contradiction in that Korihor has admitted his error and now sees the truth but he is not forgiven and restored.

True believers are called Christians in 73 BC according to Alma 46:13–15. The Bible says that this term was first used to describe believers in Antioch after the death of Jesus (Acts 11:26).

The leader of the Lamanites whose name is Amalickiah forbids his armies from attacking the city of Nephihah (Alma 51:25). However, in the next verse, the city of Nephihah is listed among the cities that the Lamanites took from the Nephites. Either this is a contradiction, or there is much that needs to be said to clarify how this happened. Apparently, the city of Nephihah was attacked by the Lamanites because Alma 52:4 says that all of the cities taken by the Lamanites were taken with great loss of blood.

22 The question is *when* the Father had given them to the Son.

23 We believe the Holy Ghost is a personified, male God who has not yet received a body. His Spirit resides in a single location but the influence of his spirit or the "it" possesses an omnipresent quality.

The term "epistle" is used to describe letters written by Moroni to the Lamanite King Ammoron around 63 BC (Alma 54:4,14). Epistles are formal letters that became an important form of communication in the Greek-speaking world as early as 300 BC. Therefore, it is highly unlikely that this term would be known among the Nephites and Lamanites in the Americas since they left almost 300 years earlier. It seems more likely that the author of the book of Alma wrote this book after the New Testament epistles were written.

THE BOOK OF HELAMAN

In the fortieth year of the reign of the judges, a serious contention arose over who should succeed Pahoran as chief judge and governor. Three of his sons: Pahoran, Paanachi, and Pacumoni were the chief contenders. When it became evident that Pahoran would be the next judge, the followers of Paanachi sent Kishkumen who murdered Pahoran. After this, Pacumoni was appointed chief judge and governor. An army of Lamanites led by Coriantumr (a dissenter from among the Nephites), attacks, and takes the City of Zarahemla. Coriantumr kills Pacumoni and marches to take the City Bountiful. Most of the Nephite armies are stationed in the cities near the borders. Lehi and Moronihah lead Nephite armies that surround the Lamanite invaders. Coriantumr is killed in the ensuing battle and the Lamanite army is defeated.

Helaman's son named Helaman becomes chief judge. Kishkumen, who is a member of a band of robbers and assassins, tries to murder Helaman but his plans are discovered and he is killed. Gadianton becomes the leader of the robber band of Kishkumen. Gadianton and his followers flee to the wilderness to escape from Helaman.

In the forty-sixth year of the judges, a great contention arose among the Nephites that caused many of them to leave the land of Zarahemla and migrate northward a great distance. They settled in lands called desolate because of the lack of timber. Because of the lack of timber, these people became experts in using cement to build houses.

The Nephites prosper under Helaman and many join the church being baptized "unto repentance." Those who believe in Jesus Christ are able to pass through the gate of heaven. There is peace and great joy in the land of Zarahemla until pride enters the hearts of those who call themselves Christians but really are not of the Church of God.

Helaman dies in the fifty-third year of the judges. He is succeeded by his son Nephi. The next year the dissentions within the church become so severe that "there was much bloodshed and the rebellious part were slain and driven out of the land" (Hel 4:2). Those who fled to the Lamanites stirred them up to war. They invaded and captured the Land of Zarahemla. Moronihah leads the Nephites who recapture half the lands taken by the Lamanites. There is great loss among the Nephites due to their wickedness. The Nephites repent of their wickedness in response to the preaching of Moronihah, Nephi, and Lehi. The people recall the prophesies of Alma and Mosiah and fear the Lamanites because they are weak.

Nephi gives up the chief judgment seat to Cezoram due to the wickedness of the people. Nephi and Lehi preach the word of God for the rest of their lives. They recall the teachings of their father Helaman that "there is no other way nor means whereby man can be saved, only through the atoning blood of Jesus Christ" (Hel 5:9). They travel among the Nephites and Lamanites preaching with great power. They are taken by an army of the Lamanites and thrown into prison. After many days, the Lamanites go to the prison to kill them but find them surrounded by fire. Nephi and Lehi are in the midst of the fire but are not burned. A great cloud of darkness engulfs those in prison and a voice tells them not to harm Nephi and Lehi. There are several earthquakes while they hear the voice.

One witness called Abinadab sees that the faces of Nephi and Lehi are shining like those of angels. Abinadab tells the people present to repent and have faith in Jesus to remove the cloud of darkness. Those who do this are each surrounded by fire and see angels descending from heaven to minister to them. This happens to about three hundred people who then go preaching among the Lamanites. The Lamanites who believe these witnesses reject the traditions of their ancestors and lay down their arms. These converts give the Nephites back the lands that they had taken.

The righteousness of the Lamanites surpasses that of the Nephites. Many of the Lamanite converts preach among the Nephites. The Nephites and Lamanites are at peace and travel freely among their lands. The Nephites and Lamanites grow prosperous. In the sixty-sixth year of the judges, Cezoram is murdered by an unknown person while sitting on the judgment seat. A member of the band of robbers and murderers led by Gadianton is responsible. This evil band grows strong and develops secret signs, words, oaths, and covenants.

The Nephites decrease because of their wickedness while the Lamanites increase as their knowledge and obedience to God's commandments grows. The Lamanites hunt down and destroy the robbers of Gadianton while the Nephites support these robbers. Nephi returns to the land of Zarahemla from the Nephite lands to the north. He is sad to see the rampant wickedness among the Nephites. Nephi calls on the people to repent or they will be destroyed.

Influential men who are judges and secret members of the band of Gadianton rise up against Nephi. They stir up the people and encourage them to reject and kill Nephi. However, a greater number of people defend him and keep him safe. Nephi tells the Nephites that their chief judge has been murdered by his brother. Five men rush to see if what Nephi says is true. They find the chief judge murdered just as Nephi said and fall down in fear and astonishment. These men are accused of killing the judge and are cast into prison. Other judges accuse Nephi of plotting to kill the chief judge with another person who committed the crime to make it look like Nephi predicted it. The people are divided about what to do with Nephi but eventually leave him alone.

God speaks to Nephi and gives him power to forgive sins by authority to seal and loose on earth and heaven. Nephi tells the people to repent or they will be smitten unto destruction. The people are so divided regarding Nephi and his teachings that they begin to kill each other. Wars among the Nephites increase until Nephi prays to God for a famine in the land to stir up the people to remember the Lord their God and repent and turn towards him. After thousands perish, the people ask Nephi to pray to God that the famine would end. "When Nephi saw that the people had repented and did humble themselves in sackcloth, he cried again to the Lord." God ends the famine and the people "esteem him as a great prophet, and a man of God, having great power and authority given unto him from God" (Hel 11:18). Peace and prosperity return to both the Nephites and Lamanites. The robbers of Gadianton increase in numbers in the wilderness and mountains such that even the armies of the Nephites and Lamanites cannot destroy them.

The Nephites return to wickedness while the Lamanites strictly observe the commandments of God according to the Law of Moses. Samuel, a Lamanite, goes to the land of Zarahemla and preaches to the people. He says that destruction awaits them within four hundred years if they do not repent and put their faith in Jesus Christ. He predicts that the Son of God will come in five years to redeem those who believe in him. The sign of his coming shall be great lights in heaven such that, in the night before he comes, it will be as it is day. A new star shall appear and there will be "many signs and wonders in heaven" (Hel 14:6).

Samuel teaches, "whosoever shall believe on the Son of God, the same shall have everlasting life" (Hel 14:8). He tells them that mankind must be redeemed from spiritual death caused by the fall of Adam and that this redemption comes only because of the resurrection of Christ. The sign of his death is total darkness for three days until Jesus rises from the dead. "There shall be great tempests, and there shall be many mountains laid low, like unto a valley, and there shall be many places which are now called valleys which shall become mountains" (Hel 14:23). Many dead saints shall be resurrected and will appear to many. These signs and wonders shall happen all across the land so that there should be no unbelief for whosoever believes shall be saved (Hel 14:28–29).

Those who believe the words of Samuel confess their sins and desire to be baptized. Those who do not believe throw rocks and shoot arrows at him but they cannot harm him because he is protected by the Spirit of the Lord. Those who wish to harm him attempt to arrest him but he flees from the land of the Nephites.

In the ninetieth year of the judges, "angels did appear unto men, wise men, and did declare unto them glad tidings of great joy" (Hel 16:14). Nevertheless, most of the Nephites and Lamanites harden their hearts. Despite the signs and wonders, Satan has a strong hold on the people. They do not believe that it is reasonable for the Son of God to come as a man and question that he should appear to them and in Jerusalem.

AUTHOR COMMENTS

Many Nephites migrate northward around 49 BC to lands without much timber. They become experts in building with cement and build many cities of wood and cement. They also keep many records including books, which are handed down through generations. They build synagogues, temples and many other types of buildings throughout the land (Hel 3:8–9). Based on this account and archeological evidence, the Mayans are the only civilization in the American continent that can fit this description.[24] However, the Mayan archeological evidence does

---

24   This argument posits that all that can be discovered has been discovered. It also does not take into account the events of 3 Ne 8:1–18 where much evidence was lost. This passage records great earthquakes and storms that followed the crucifixion of Jesus such that many cities were destroyed.

not indicate any connection with the Nephites. Among the many problems are:

1. Mayan writings do not mention anything about the Nephites or their history as recorded in the *Book of Mormon*.
2. There is no evidence that the Mayans knew the Mosaic Laws and believed in many gods.
3. There are no records that Mayan society was organized based on judges and prophets around this time.
4. The Mayan civilization began 2000–3000 BC, which is at least 1000 years before Lehi arrived.
5. The Mayans practiced human sacrifice and bloodletting, which are not mentioned in the *Book of Mormon*.
6. The Mayan and Nephite calendars were different with the former based on eighteen months of 20 days versus 12 months for the Nephites.

Helaman 3:27–28 says that God is merciful to all those who have sincere faith in Jesus Christ. Helaman says that whoever believes in Jesus will have eternal life. These verses, that teach that salvation is by faith alone, conflict with others that say that salvation is by faith plus works. (Mosiah 2:41; 4:6–7; 4:30). Furthermore, these verses conflict with Mosiah 3:11, which says that all men go to heaven except for those who knowingly break God's commandments. Samuel teaches, "the resurrection of Christ redeemeth mankind, yea, even all mankind" (Hel 14:17). In summary, there are verses that indicate salvation is by faith alone, faith, and works, and that all men are saved (even those who have no faith in Jesus) except those who willingly reject Jesus and break his commandments.

The prophet Samuel predicts that there will be three days of total darkness on the earth following the death of Jesus. The sun, moon, and stars will not be visible until Jesus rises from the dead. Further signs include great storms and shifts in the earth that will make many mountains valleys and vice versa. Historical records do not reflect that there were three days of darkness or that there were widespread shifts in the elevation of the surface of the earth associated with the death of Jesus.[25] Given the magnitude and severity of such changes, it is highly unlikely that there is no historic or geologic evidence to support them.

I agree that historical records are subject to change with new discoveries. However, I believe we have to rely on what is known from historical records or else an equally untenable position is reached where these records are not considered reliable because they do not support a point of view.

Helaman 16:14 says that angels appeared to wise men at the birth of Jesus: "And angels did appear unto men, wise men, and did declare unto them glad tidings of great joy." The Bible says that angels appeared to shepherds the night of Jesus birth (Luke 2:8-14). It is possible that the text of Helaman could mean that the men (shepherds according to the Bible) to whom the angels appeared were wise. However, the words "wise men" following "men" appears to refer to those who were exceptionally wise which would not be expected of shepherds.[26]

---

25   Again, this assumes that historical records are 100% accurate, which is an untenable position.

26   Another reason a second witness is so valuable. It provides additional information.

THE THIRD BOOK OF NEPHI

Six hundred years after Lehi leaves Jerusalem, Nephi, the son of Helaman, leaves the Land of Zarahemla. He gives the plates of brass to his eldest son also named Nephi. Those who do not believe the prophecies about Jesus want to kill those who do believe. They plan to do this if the day with no night predicted by Samuel does not happen. Nephi prays to God to spare his people and, in reply, the voice of the Lord tells him that tomorrow he will come into the world. The next day when the sun sets "there was no darkness when the night came" (3 Ne 1:19). A new star appears in the sky and many people are converted.

After many years, wickedness grows among the people and they no longer believe that there will be further signs at the death of Jesus. The Gadianton robbers become numerous and lay waste many cities such that the Nephites and Lamanites unite to fight them. God removes the curse from the Lamanites and their skin becomes white like the Nephites. The Lamanites become known as Nephites. The Nephites drive the Gadianton robbers into the mountains.

The leader of the Gadianton robbers, named Giddianhi, writes an epistle to Lachoneus who is the governor of the Nephites. He demands that the Nephites surrender and join them not as slaves but as brothers. Giddianhi says that the Nephites will be destroyed without mercy if they refuse. Lachoneus refuses to surrender and sends a proclamation to the Nephites telling them to gather their possessions and assemble in one place. Thousands of Nephites gather in the Land of Zarahemla in the appointed place. He orders fortifications to be built and posts guards around the gathering place. Gidgiddoni is appointed chief judge and head of the Nephite army.

The robbers come down from the mountains and take possession of the Nephite lands but find them empty and desolate. Therefore, Giddianhi gathers the robbers and attacks the Nephites at their assembly place. A great and terrible battle ensues in which the robbers are beaten and slaughtered. Gidgiddoni commands the Nephites to pursue and slay the robbers as far as the borders of the mountains. Giddianhi is killed while fleeing to the mountains.

Two years later the robbers return and attack the Nephites but are again defeated. Their leader, Zemnarihah, is hanged. The Nephites rejoice and praise God for their deliverance. They serve God with all diligence day and night. The Nephites disperse and return to the lands they vacated. Many of their cities are rebuilt and they build highways. However, disputes arise due to the pride and great wealth of some of the people. The wealthy have greater learning and treat others with afflictions and persecutions. The chief priests, lawyers, and judges conspire to kill those who preach against the inequities among the people. They also oppose the prophets who teach about Jesus and they wish to establish a king to rule the Nephites. The chief judge is murdered and the people separate themselves into tribes and appoint their own chiefs or leaders such that the central government is destroyed. Some of the people appoint a man named Jacob to be their king.

Nephi begins to preach repentance and the remission of sins through Jesus Christ among the Nephites that are not under Jacob. Nephi preaches with power and performs many miracles. Angels minister to him daily. Thirty-four years after the birth of Jesus, a terrible storm shakes the earth. Cities sink beneath the sea while others are raised on mountains such that the whole face of the land is changed. Many cities are burned or shaken until their buildings are destroyed. These destructions last for about three hours and are followed by darkness. The darkness is such that no light is seen or can be kindled for three days. The people mourn and groan because of the darkness and destruction.

A voice is heard "among all the inhabitants of the earth, upon all the face of this land" that says judgment is come upon them because of their sins (3 Ne 9:1–2). The City of Gadiomnah which is inhabited by the people of King Jacob is burned with fire because they destroyed "the peace of my people and the government of the land" (3 Ne 9:9). The voice says that he is Jesus Christ and that "if ye will come unto me ye shall have eternal life" (3 Ne 9:14). Jesus says that those who receive him will become sons of God and will be redeemed. He tells them to repent and come to him as little children.

The people mourn for three days in total darkness because of the loss of their kindred and friends. The righteous people are saved from the whirlwind, movements of the earth and fire. Jesus descends from heaven and appears to the righteous who are gathered around the temple in the Land of Bountiful. Jesus invites them to thrust their hands into his side and feel the nail prints in his hands. Each person does this and then falls down and worships Jesus. Nephi and eleven others are called by Jesus and given power to baptize by immersion in the name of the Father, the Son, and the Holy Ghost. Jesus says, "whoso believeth in me and is baptized, the same shall be saved; and they are they who shall inherit the kingdom of God" (3 Ne 11:33). Those who are baptized "shall be visited with fire and with the Holy Ghost, and shall receive remission of their sins" (3 Ne 12:2).

Jesus tells them to "come unto me and be saved; for verily I say unto you, that except ye shall keep my commandments, which I have commanded you at this time, ye shall in no case enter into the kingdom of heaven" (3 Ne 12:20). He instructs them regarding sins such as anger, adultery, and swearing. Jesus commands them to love their enemies and return good for evil in order to be perfect like Jesus and the Father. Jesus says that he is the lawgiver and the fulfillment of the Mosaic laws. "Look unto me and endure to the end, and ye shall live; for unto him that endureth to the end will I give eternal life" (3 Ne 15:9).

Jesus heals the sick and prays with the people to the Father. He eats bread and wine with them commanding them to do this in remembrance of him. Jesus finishes instructing them and he touches each of his twelve disciples enabling them to "give the Holy Ghost" to others (3 Ne 18:36–37). They are enveloped by a cloud and Jesus ascends to heaven.

The next day, the people gather to pray and await the return of Jesus from heaven. Nephi and the others chosen by Jesus are baptized and are filled with the Holy Ghost. They are encircled by fire and angels come down from heaven to minister to them. Jesus also comes from heaven and stands among them. He prays to the Father while the assembly also prays. Jesus appears exceedingly white and those praying with him are also transformed. Jesus miraculously produces bread and wine for a large number of people. He tells them that Gentiles who believe in Jesus will be numbered among the house of Israel. A city called New Jerusalem will be built and Jesus will be there.

Whoever listens to Jesus, repents, and is baptized will be saved. Jesus predicts that a day will come when the wicked will be burned with fire. Elijah will be sent "before the coming of the great and dreadful day of the Lord" (3 Ne 25:5). The elements of the earth shall melt with "fervent heat" and the earth and heavens will pass away" (3 Ne 26:3). Everyone shall stand before God and be judged by their works. Those whose works are good shall be resurrected to eternal life while those whose works are evil will be resurrected to damnation. Jesus preaches many things for three days and performs many miracles. Those who are baptized are filled with the Holy Ghost.

Jesus appears to his disciples while they are fasting and praying. He tells them to repent and be baptized in his name and endure to the end. Those who do not endure to the end will be "hewn down and cast into the fire" (3 Ne 27:17). Jesus asks each of his disciples "What is it that you desire of me, before I go to the Father" (3 Ne 28:1). The disciples reply that they want to live a full life of ministry and then speedily enter the kingdom of God. Jesus tells them that they will live to be seventy-two years old and then find rest. Three disciples wish Jesus to grant that they would never taste death. Jesus replies that they will never die, but be transformed in the twinkling of an eye upon his return. Until then, they will continue to bring souls to Jesus as long as the world endures.

Jesus ascends to heaven and the disciples are "caught up into heaven" where they see and hear unspeakable things (3 Ne 28:13). The disciples return to the earth where many are converted through their preaching. Mormon says that the three disciples will go among the Gentiles and Jews but they will not recognize them. They will "minister unto all the scattered tribes of Israel, and unto all nations, kindreds, tongues, and peoples" (3 Ne 28:29). Jesus continues in this verse to say that these three disciples will bring many to faith through the "convincing power of God which is in them." Mormon invites the Gentiles to turn from their wicked ways, to repent, and be baptized. If they do this, they will be filled with the Holy Ghost and be numbered among the people who are of the House of Israel.

AUTHOR COMMENTS

Zedekiah was the king of Judah when the Babylonians destroyed Jerusalem in 586 BC. Zedekiah reigned as king for eleven years before his defeat (2 Chronicles 36:11). Therefore, his reign began in 597 BC. According to 3 Ne 1:1, Lehi left Jerusalem in the first year of Zedekiah's reign 600 years before the birth of Jesus or 600 BC.[27]

3 Nephi 1:19 says that the night that Jesus is born, the sun sets

---

27   This may have been a mere matter of approximation.

but it remains light: "There was no darkness in all that night, but it was as light as though it was mid-day." In the Bible, Jesus is born at night and there is no unusual daylight (Luke 2:7–8).

The Lamanites who converted unto the Lord join the Nephites against the Gadianton robbers. These Lamanites become known as Nephites and God removes their curse, which causes their skin to become white like the Nephites. The idea that skin color is associated with God's blessings and curses is not found in the Bible.[28]

3 Nephi 7:25 says that baptism is "a witness and testimony before God, and unto the people" of repentance and the forgiveness of sins. This verse indicates that baptism is a way to show that there has been a spiritual change through faith in Jesus Christ. Therefore, baptism is not necessary for salvation but rather is an act of obedience following the command of Jesus. (Matt 28:19; Mark 16:16). However, there are other verses in the *Book of Mormon* that say baptism is essential for salvation (3 Nephi 11:33–34).[29]

The death of Jesus occurs in the thirty-fourth year after his birth. (3 Nephi 8:5). A great and terrible storm and upheavals in the earth occur when Jesus dies. These upheavals are so severe that "the whole face of the earth was changed" (3 Ne 8:12). Cities are swallowed up beneath the sea while others are thrust up on mountains. This is followed by three days of total darkness such that "there was not any light seen, neither fire, nor glimmer, neither the sun, nor the moon, nor the stars" (3 Ne 12:22). The Bible tells of darkness and an earthquake at the death of Jesus. However, there are no indications that the natural disasters are as severe, widespread, and long lasting as those mentioned in 3 Nephi. Furthermore, there is no geological evidence that suggests

---

28 Shows God's omnipotence and the value of a second witness.

29 This is a non-sequitur. Just because baptism means one thing does not disqualify it from meaning several things at the same time.

that there are mountains in the Americas that are two thousand years old.[30]

Jesus says "except ye shall keep my commandments, which I commanded you at this time, ye shall in no case enter into the kingdom of heaven" (3 Ne 12:20). This suggests that salvation can only be attained by keeping the law and the commandments. This idea is also evident in 3 Nephi 27:17 which says "he that endureth not unto the end, the same is he that is also hewn down and cast into the fire from whence they can no more return." These statements conflict with the Bible and many other verses in the *Book of Mormon* that say salvation is by faith in Jesus Christ and is not based on works. The idea of faith plus works is found in 3 Nephi 15:9 which says "Look unto me and endure unto the end, and ye shall live for unto him that endureth to the end will I give eternal life." This verse also stresses that faith and good works must be a way of life until death, which implies that it is possible to lose salvation if both are not always present. It is apparent that there is not consistency in the *Book of Mormon* regarding what is necessary to enter heaven.[31]

Three of the twelve Nephite disciples chosen by Jesus ask that they would never die. Jesus grants their request and says that they will continue to minister to the scattered Jews around the world as well as "all nations, kindreds, tongues and people" (3 Ne 28:29). Jesus tells these three disciples that they will bring many souls to Jesus. When Jesus returns on the final judgment day, they will be changed "in the twinkling of an eye from mortality to immortality" (3 Ne 28:8). These disciples can't be tempted by Satan because they are sanctified in the flesh such that they are holy. Certainly, such exceptional men ministering in the name of Jesus and the power of the Holy Spirit throughout the world over

---

30   Doesn't mean it won't be discovered in the future.

31   There is great consistency. It takes faith and works, but preachers and prophets usually focus on one sermon/subject at a time. As the Bible says: "For we know in part and we prophesy in part" (1Cor 13:9).

the past two thousand years would be known.[32] Certainly many souls would have come to Jesus because of the convincing power of God within them. (3 Nephi 28:29). According to 3 Nephi 28:30–31, these three men still walk the earth performing many miracles and awaiting the second coming of Jesus. However, these three men have no names nor does history attest to their exceptional holiness and miraculous powers among men.[33]

---

32   Would they? Is *(the apostle)* John known? This assertion limits both the extraordinary nature of these four men and their unique mission, not to mention the omnipotent purposes of God.

33   Which makes it all the more believable. Were such men to come forward and reveal their true mission, they would almost certainly be imposters. And even if they weren't, who would believe some guys who made such a claim. It is God's will they remain anonymous until he wills otherwise.

THE FOURTH BOOK OF NEPHI

In 36 AD, all the people (both Nephites and Lamanites) are "converted unto the Lord" (4 Ne 1:2). There are no contentions or disputes and everyone holds everything in common, such that there are no rich or poor, no bond or free people. The disciples perform many miracles such as healing the sick and raising the dead. The people prosper and walk "after the commandments they had received from their Lord and their God" (4 Ne 1:12). This state of peace, prosperity, and harmony lasts one hundred and ten years.

Some of the people revolt and call themselves Lamanites. In 201 AD, the Nephites begin to deny the true church of Christ. Churches arose that "professed to know the Christ, and yet they did deny the more parts of his gospel" (4 Ne 1a; 27). Another church arose that denied Jesus and persecuted the true church. They put the three witnesses in prison but the prisons "were rent in twain" (4 Ne 1:30). The three witnesses go forth doing mighty miracles. Despite the miracles, the people want to destroy them so they cast them into a fiery furnace and to wild beasts without harming them.

The number of people faithful to Christ dwindles until by 231 AD "a great division happens among the people" (4 Ne 1:35). Those that believe in Christ become the Nephites and those who do not become Lamanites. The Lamanites teach their children to hate the Nephites. By 306 AD, the Nephites and Lamanites both become wicked and so resemble each other. The robbers of

Gadianton arise and spread throughout the land. There are no righteous people left, except for the three Disciples of Christ, and Ammaron, the keeper of the sacred records. In 320 AD, Ammaron hides the sacred records until "they might come again unto the remnant of the house of Jacob" (4 Ne 1:49).

AUTHOR COMMENTS

The people grow in wickedness despite the presence of the three Disciples of Christ who continue to minister and perform miracles. This decline continues for three hundred years until all the people are wicked except for the three witnesses and Ammaron who is the keeper of the sacred records. This seems contrary to 3 Nephi 28:29, which says that the three witnesses shall minister throughout the earth and bring many to Christ "because of the convincing power of God which is in them."[34]

---

34 However, the will of three semi-mortals isn't going to change the natural course that runs according to the immortal will and power of God.

THE BOOK OF MORMON

Ammaron tells Mormon that he has hidden the sacred records in a hill called Shim in the land of Antum. He instructs Mormon to remove the plates of Nephi but to leave the other sacred records. About a year later, war breaks out between the Nephites and the Lamanites. The Nephites win several battles but wickedness increases until the Lord removes the beloved disciples. Consequently, miracles and healings cease among the people. Jesus visits Mormon when he is fifteen and tells him not to preach to the people because of their rebellious ways.

The Nephites appoint Mormon to lead their armies when he is sixteen. The Lamanites attack and the Nephites flee to the City of Angola. The Lamanites drive the Nephites out of the City of Angola. The Nephites gather their forces and defeat the Lamanites. There are many robbers, thieves, and murderers throughout the land. The Nephites refuse to repent and turn to God. Mormon leads the Nephites to victory over the Lamanites and robbers of Gadianton. The land is divided with the Nephites taking the lands northward of a narrow passage.

Mormon tells the Nephites that they must repent, be baptized and build up the church and then God will be with them. However, the Nephites do not listen. The King of the Lamanites sends Mormon an epistle that warns him that they are about to attack. Mormon gathers the Nephite armies and fortifies the City of Desolation, which is near the border of the Lamanite lands. The Lamanites attack the City of Desolation and are defeated.

The Nephites become proud of their victories boasting of their own strength and not acknowledging God. Mormon refuses to lead them when they decide to invade Lamanite lands. The Nephites are defeated and are driven back to the City of Desolation where they are also defeated. The Nephites flee to the City of Teancum. The Nephites and Lamanites continue to fight driving each other back and forth, as they sometimes win and other times loose battles. In 375 AD, the Lamanites attack with all their power and from this time forward, the Nephites are beaten.

Mormon again takes command of the Nephite armies. He writes an epistle to the King of the Lamanites requesting, "that we might gather together our people unto the land of Cumorah "to a hill which is also called Cumorah where they would stand and fight (Morm 6:2). The King of the Lamanites grants Mormon's request. Mormon hides the sacred records in the hill of Cumorah except for a few plates that he gives to his son Moroni. The Lamanites attack and Mormon is wounded. The Nephites are destroyed except for twenty-four survivors including Mormon and Moroni.

Mormon speaks to the Lamanites and the remaining Nephites. He tells them that they must repent and believe in Jesus Christ. He says that Jesus, the Father, and the Holy Ghost are one God. The Lamanites kill Mormon and Moroni writes that the Lamanites begin to war among themselves after the Nephites are destroyed. Moroni predicts that the sacred records will be found in a day of darkness when "the power of God shall be denied and churches become defiled" (Morm 8:28). He says that churches will pronounce that people's sins are forgiven in exchange for money. People will become full of pride and love money rather than those in need.

Moroni says that unbelievers would be more miserable dwelling with God under a consciousness of their filthiness before him than they would be to dwell with the dammed in hell. When unbelievers appear before God, the holiness of Jesus will kindle a flame of unquenchable fire upon them. Moroni pleads that unbelievers would cry out to the Father in the name of Jesus that they might be "cleansed by the blood of the Lamb, at that great and last day" (Morm 9:6). Moroni preaches, "he that believeth and is baptized shall be saved, but he that believeth not shall be dammed" (Morm 9:23).

AUTHOR COMMENTS

Mormon is wounded and captured by the Lamanites following the battle of Cumorah. Mormon 6:10 says that the Lamanites "passed by me that they did not put an end to my life." In Mormon Chapter 7, he addresses the Lamanites and the remnant of the Nephites. Mormon tells them to repent and believe in Jesus Christ so that it shall be well with them in the day of judgment. His son Moroni says that his father "was killed by them (the Lamanites) and I even remain alone to write the sad tale of the destruction of my people" (Morm 8:3). Thus, it appears that Mormon survived the battle but was later killed by the Lamanites. This view is also supported by Moroni who is uncertain about whether the Lamanites will also kill him. However, this appears to be contrary to Mormon 8:5 in which Moroni says that his father "hath been slain in battle."

Moroni says that on the final day of judgment, that unbelievers will no longer be able to deny Christ and their consciences will be tormented by guilt (Morm 9:3). So great is the torment of their guilt that they will be better suffering in hell than being with God because a "flame of unquenchable fire" will come upon them (Morm 9:5). This seems to contradict the LDS teaching that few people will be dammed to hell and that some of those in hell will accept Jesus and enter the Telestial kingdom.[35]

---

35 A unique aspect of Mormon doctrine involves the concept of Eternal Progression. This posits that our souls are not finished or at their terminus of growth at death. Far from it. Joseph Smith has said it will be a great while after passing through the veil (of death) before we will have learned them all (the

The LDS doctrine of Eternal Progression after death conflicts with the cited verses in Alma 34:32–34 which state that it is only during this life that men can do good works to prepare for eternal life. This can only be reconciled by claiming both to be true and thus a paradox beyond our understanding. Alma 29:4 says that God grants men salvation or destruction, as they will. This is only partly true. God does judge according to the choices we make but without his grace the Bible teaches that mankind is not capable of choosing salvation (Eph 2:1–9). Furthermore, it appears that the souls of at least those in the Telestial and Terrestrial kingdoms will not continue to progress to godhood (D&C 76:112; 84:74). Those who go to the two lower levels of the Celestial kingdom also do not appear eligible to progress to godhood as they become angels which are ministering spirits to those in the highest level of the Celestial kingdom(D&C 132:16–17).

---

lessons of salvation and exaltation). Nevertheless, this is another example of the paradoxical quality of truth. (e.g., Alma 34:32–34). Which truism is right? They both are! In the end, it comes down to what each person most desires eternally (e.g., Alma 29:4). God is perfectly fair.

THE BOOK OF ETHER

Moroni relates the history of the Jaredites based on twenty-four plates found by the people of Limhi. Jared and his brother find favor with the Lord who leads them with their families to "a land which is choice above all the lands of the earth" (Ether 1:42). God promises that their descendants will be great among the nations "upon all the face of the earth" (Ether 1:43). The Jaredites build barges as God directs them. The barges are so tight that there is no light inside them. The finger of God touches some clear stones gathered by Jared and they provide light for the Jaredites inside the barges.

The Lord shows himself to the brother of Jared and says "never have I showed myself unto men whom I have created, for never has men believed in me as thou hast" (Ether 3:15). Jesus instructs the brother of Jared to record what he sees and hears but not to share it with anyone. The Lord shows the brother of Jared "all the inhabitants of the earth which had been, and all that would be" (Ether 3:25). The brother of Jared is told to seal up the records of his encounter with Jesus plus two of the clear stones until after "Christ should show himself unto his people" (Ether 3:28).

Moroni records "the very things which the brother of Jared saw" (Ether 4:4). He is told by Jesus that these records will not be revealed until the Gentiles "shall repent of their inequity and become clean before the Lord" (Ether 4:6). In that day, the Gentiles will have faith in Jesus and "then will I manifest unto them the things which the brother of Jared saw, even unto the unfolding unto them of all my revelations" (Ether 4:7).

The Jaredites travel to the Promised Land in eight barges. After they arrive, their families expand and the people choose Pagag, who is Jared's oldest son, to be their king. Pagag refuses to be king so another son named Orihah becomes king. Orihah rules in righteousness for many years. His son Corihor rebels and takes his father captive. Further rebellions and dissensions follow such that the country is divided into two kingdoms.

The people revile the prophets but King Shule supports them so the people are brought to repentance. King Shule begets Omer who begets Jared who rebels against his father and becomes king. Jared is deposed by his brothers Esrom and Coriantumur but is spared because he promises to reinstate their father as king. Jared later conspires to have his father murdered but Omer flees. Jared is murdered as he sits upon his throne and his son Akish becomes king. Akish and his sons fight each other until only thirty people are left. Omer is restored as king and begets Emer who succeeds him.

Emer rules for sixty-two years and the people prosper having cattle, swine, horses, asses, elephants, cureloms and cumoms. Omer's son Coriantum succeeds him and his son Corian succeeds Coriantum. Corn is the son of Coriantum who succeeds him. Corn is killed by his son Heth. King Heth and his people ignore the prophets and so they suffer drought, famine, and poisonous snakes. The people repent of their sins and cry out to God who ends the plagues. Shez succeeds Heth and follows the ways of the Lord. He is succeeded by Riplakish who "did not do which was right in the sight of the Lord for he did have many wives and concubines" (Ether 10:5). Riplakish taxes the people to build spacious buildings. The people revolt and kill Riplakish but his son Morianton gathers an army and becomes king. The kingdom passes from one to another through wars, deceit, and intrigue.

The prophets predict the destruction of the Jaredites unless they repent of their wickedness. The people reject the words of the prophets so wars and destruction befall them. The prophet Ether says that the promised land of the Jaredites is the "place of the New Jerusalem which would come down out of heaven, and the holy sanctuary of the Lord" (Ether 13:3). The people cast Ether out so he dwells in a cavity of a rock. Wars follow among the Jaredites such that the bodies of men, women, and children are strewn across the land with none to bury them. Millions of people are killed in continuing wars between the supporters of Shiz and Coriantumr. The people continue to fight until only Shiz and Coriantumr remain. Coriantumr kills Shiz and is the last of the Jaredites as Ether predicted.

AUTHOR COMMENTS

In Ether 1:43, God promises Jared and his brother that the greatest nation on the face of the earth will arise from their descendants. This would happen after they reached the Promised Land. The Book of Ether says that the Jaredites grew to millions of people in the Promised Land. However, there is no archeological or historical evidence of the Jaredites in the Americas. Furthermore, the Jaredites kill each other through wars until only Coriantumr is left so it seems the Jaredites never became the greatest nation on the face of the earth.[36] Evidence of great civilizations such as the Egyptian pyramids still exists and it is hard to imagine that this civilization was greater.

The people prosper while Emer is king having much food, gold and precious things as well as cattle, swine, horses, elephants, cureloms and cumoms. Limhi is the king of the Nephites around 121 BC when the plates of the Jaredites are found.

There are no skeletal remains known that support there were

---

36   The promise is that they would be the greatest nation up to that time. Three thousand years can wipe out such evidence especially if they were not skilled in stonework.

many cattle, swine, horses, and elephants in the Americas more than one hundred years before the birth of Christ. There are no historical records to suggest that these animals were introduced to the Americas before the time of Christ. Horses were introduced to the Americas by the Spanish in the 16th century. According to the *Book of Mormon*, curelomes and cumoms are animals that are useful to man but it is unknown what these animals are.[37]

The LDS Church practiced polygamy between 1831 and 1890. Today some splinter sects that call themselves Mormon-Fundamentalists have more than one wife, which contradicts Ether 10:5 that says that King Riplakish did evil in the sight of God because he had many wives. The LDS Church itself no longer practices or condones polygamy, including the practice of it by these excommunicated splinter sects.

---

37   This is evidence of the *Book of Mormon's* originality.

THE BOOK OF MORONI

Moroni flees for his life as the Lamanites kill any Nephites that do not deny Jesus as the Christ. Moroni writes that the apostles are given the power to impute the presence of the Holy Ghost upon anyone they wish by the laying on of their hands. The apostles ordain priests and teachers by laying their hands on them and praying in the name of Jesus. The priests and elders administer the sacramental bread and wine praying that God would sanctify them and that they would eat and drink in remembrance of the body and blood of Jesus.

Moroni writes "a few of the words of my father Mormon" which he taught the people in the synagogue (Moro 7:1). Mormon teaches that evil men can't do good in God's view. He quotes Jesus as saying "Repent all ye ends of the earth, and come to me, and be baptized in my name and have faith in me, that ye may be saved" (Moro 7:34). Little children do not need to be baptized because "the curse of Adam is taken from them...by the death and resurrection of Jesus Christ" (Moro 8:8). Repentance and baptism are to be taught to adults "who are accountable and capable of committing sin" (Moro 8:10). Since little children can't repent, "it is awful wickedness to deny the pure mercies of God unto them for they are alive in him (Jesus) because of his mercy" (Moro 8:19). Little children are "alive in Christ" and are not under the law such that they can't be condemned by their actions (Moro 8:22).

Mormon bemoans the wickedness of both the Nephites and Lamanites. Moroni exhorts mankind not to deny the gifts of God.

They should "come unto Christ" and be perfected in him "being sanctified by the grace of God through the shedding of the blood of Christ" (Moro 10:32). Moroni concludes by saying farewell. He says his spirit goes to paradise to rest until it is reunited with his body at the final judgment.

AUTHOR COMMENTS

Moroni says that repentance, faith in Jesus and baptism are required for salvation. (Moroni 7:34). As we have previously seen, this contradicts many places in the Bible and the *Book of Mormon* (Table 1). Infant baptism is called wickedness and is prohibited by Moroni but is not explicitly forbidden by the Bible.[38] The Bible provides many examples of adults being baptized after believing in Jesus (Acts 2:41; 8:12–13; 8:35–38 and 16:31–33). There are no explicit examples of infants being baptized in the Bible but a case can be made that this may have happened when whole households were converted (Acts 16:15; 16:33). Thus, the Biblical pattern is for baptism to be a conscious decision by those who have repented of their sins and have placed their faith in Jesus as their personal Savior and Lord.[39] In his farewell, Moroni says that he will remain a spirit until the resurrection (Moro 10:34). How does he take the plates from Joseph Smith if he is a spirit?

---

38   Thus the need of a second witness to clarify truth.

39   Yes. The two records agree on this.

THE DOCTRINE AND COVENANTS

Joseph Smith receives a revelation from God in which the Lord warns of a coming judgment day. Joseph and those whom God gives his commandments have power to lay the foundation of a new church. They are to bring it forth out of obscurity and darkness. It will be the only true and living church upon the face of the earth (D&C 1:30). Those who repent and keep the commandments of God will be forgiven. The priesthood of this church will be revealed by Elijah the prophet "before the coming of the great and dreadful day of the Lord" (D&C 2:1).

God chastens Joseph for "transgressing the commandment I gave you" by giving sacred translations to a wicked man (D&C 3:10–12). He is told that his gift of translation of the sacred plates will be taken away if he does not repent. God enters a covenant with Joseph "and those persons to whom I commanded you" to translate the sacred plates and "deliver my word unto the children of men" (D&C 5:6). God says Joseph will have eternal life if he "remains firm in keeping the commandments where with I have commanded you" (D&C 5:22). God tells Joseph to seek wisdom rather than riches and "the mysteries of God shall be unfolded unto you" (D&C 6:7). He will be saved if he remains faithful to the end.

Oliver Cowdery is also given the gift of translation and "the gift of Aaron" as well. Oliver will also inherit the kingdom of heaven if he keeps God's commandments (D&C 8:1-6). The apostle

John will not die until Jesus returns in glory. John will "prophesy before nations, kindreds, tongues, and peoples" (D&C 7:3).

Some of the translations are entrusted to wicked men who alter them in order to destroy God's work. Satan inspires these men to challenge Joseph to do another translation of the works that they altered. They plan to discredit him by showing that he has no gift from God by contrasting the second translation to their altered version. God tells Joseph not to retranslate the stolen pages but to translate the remainder of the plates of Nephi.

Hyrum Smith, who is the brother of Joseph, is told to seek wisdom instead of riches. He is to first seek to study God's words and not to preach until he is called. "As many as receive me (Jesus), to them will I give the power to become the sons of God, even to them that believe in my name" (D&C 11:30).

Joseph Smith and Oliver Cowdery receive the Priesthood of Aaron by the hands of an angel who identifies himself as John the Baptist. They receive "the keys of the ministering of angels, and the gospel of repentance, and of baptism by immersion for the remission of sins" (D&C 13:1). Those who keep God's commandments and endure to the end will have eternal life. Oliver Cowdery, David Whitmer, and Martin Harris see the sacred plates, the breastplate, the sword of Laban and the Urim and Thummim given to Jared. They are to preach repentance because those who repent, are baptized in Jesus name, and endure until the end will be saved (D&C 18:22).

Jesus will judge everyone according to his or her deeds. Every person must repent or suffer endless torment, which does not mean that there will be no end to this torment (D&C 19:6–7). This is because Endless is a name of God and so describes the punishment of God not the permanent state of punishment (D&C 19:10). Jesus commands, "thou shalt not covet thy neighbor's wife, nor seek thy neighbor's life" (D&C 19:25). Jesus says do not covet property but "impart it freely to the printing of the *Book of Mormon*" (D&C 19:26). They are to pray "and declare repentance and faith on the Savior, and the remission of sins by baptism and by fire, yea, even the Holy Ghost" (D&C 19:31).

In the year 1830, the Church of Christ is "organized and established agreeable to the laws of our country, by the will of God" (D&C 20:1). Joseph Smith and Oliver Cowdery are ordained apostles of Jesus Christ and become the first and second elders of the church. Those who receive their record of the fullness of the gospel of Jesus Christ in faith and work righteousness shall receive a crown of eternal life.

God is the same "yesterday, today and forever. Amen" (D&C 20:12). God is infinite and eternal and unchangeable. (D&C 20:17).

Mankind has transgressed God's holy laws and so everyone is in a fallen state. God sent his only begotten son to be crucified and rise from the dead. He ascended into heaven "to reign with almighty power according to the will of the Father. That as many as would believe and be baptized in his holy name and endure in faith to the end should be saved" (D&C 20:24–25). Those who lived before the birth of Christ have eternal life based on their faith in the words of the prophets. The Father, Son, and Holy Ghost are one God, infinite and eternal, without end (D&C 20:28). Justification and sanctification are through the grace of Jesus Christ. However, it is possible for a man to "fall from grace and depart from the living God" (D&C 20:32).

Those who desire to be baptized must come with broken hearts and contrite spirits. They must truly repent of their sins and take upon themselves the name of Jesus Christ "to serve him to the end and truly manifest by their works that they have received of the Spirit of Christ" (D&C 20:37). Baptized church members must show by a godly walk and conversation that they are worthy of their membership. Infants and children must not be baptized. Only those who are accountable before God for their actions and capable of repentance may be baptized. Baptisms are only to be performed by those who are authorized and they must be by immersion in the name of the Father, Son, and Holy Ghost.

Apostles are elders and they are to baptize; ordain other elders, priests, teachers and deacons as well as administer communion (D&C 20:38–40).

Church members are to meet often "to partake of bread and wine in the remembrance of the Lord Jesus" (D&C 20:75). Members of the church who are "overtaken in a fault, shall be dealt with as the scriptures direct" (D&C 20:80). A list of the members of the church shall be kept in a book by one of the elders.

Joseph Smith and Oliver Cowdery ordain each other by laying their hands on each other. Joseph is called a seer, translator, prophet, apostle, and elder. All the previous covenants are "done away in this thing; and this is a new and everlasting covenant" (D&C 22:1). Those who wish to become members must be baptized in the Mormon Church even if they were previously baptized. Baptisms performed by other churches are called "dead works" (D&C 22:2).

God tells Emma Smith "those who receive my gospel are sons and daughters of my kingdom" (D&C 25:1). She is called an elect lady whose life will be preserved if she "walk(s) in the paths of righteousness before me" (D&C 25:2). Emma is to be a scribe for her husband Joseph; be ordained to expound the scriptures; exhort the church and select sacred hymns.

Joseph Smith is compared to Moses in that only he can "receive commandments and revelations in this church" (D&C 28:2). Oliver Cowdery is to "declare faithfully the commandments and revelations with power and authority unto the church" (D&C 28:3). The city of Zion shall be built "on the borders by the Lamanites" (D&C 28:9).

Jesus shall return "with power and great glory with all the hosts thereof, and dwell in righteousness with men on earth a thousand years" (D&C 29:11). The sun will be darkened and the moon's appearance will be like blood; the stars will fall from heaven and there will be signs in heaven before the return of Jesus. God will send flies upon the face of the earth that will eat human flesh and "cause maggots to come in upon them" (D&C 29:18). The flesh of the wicked will fall off their bones and their eyes will fall out of their sockets. Wild animals will devour their flesh. When the thousand years is over, men will again deny God and then the end will come. The earth will be consumed and pass away. A new heaven and earth will be created. The righteous will be gathered to eternal life but the wicked will be cast into "everlasting fire prepared for the devil and his angels" (D&C 29:27-28).

Little children are redeemed from the foundation of the world and can't sin because they are not accountable before God. Faith in Jesus is essential for salvation. The gift of the Holy Ghost will be given to those who have faith in Jesus by the laying on of hands. Jesus "so loved the world that he gave his own life, that as many as would believe might become the sons of God" (D&C 34:3).

The gospel of Jesus is "repentance and baptism by water, and then cometh the baptism of fire and the Holy Ghost" (D&C 39:6). The elders shall go and preach the gospel of repentance and baptize with water. The elders, teachers, and priests must teach the gospel in the Bible and the *Book of Mormon*. Those who receive the Spirit by the prayer of faith are the only ones who can teach. Those in the church who steal, lie, lust, commit adultery, or other sins shall be cast out if they do not repent. Those who kill "shall not have forgiveness in this world nor in the world to come" (D&C 42:18).

Donations to the church shall be used first for the support of the bishop and then those in need. The elders and high priests "are to have their families supported out of the property which is consecrated to the bishop, for the good of the poor and for other purposes" (D&C 42:71). Every person who belongs to the Church of Christ "shall observe to keep all the commandments and covenants of the church" (D&C 42:78). Those who kill, commit adultery, steal and lie, or do anything else sinful "shall be delivered up unto the law of the land" (D&C 42:79-86).

The church is to call men to repentance until the Lord Jesus returns to the earth. His people shall reign on the earth with Jesus for a thousand years. Satan shall be bound until the thousand years is done and then he will be loosed to reign "a little season, and then cometh the end of the earth" (D&C 43:31). The righteous will be changed "in the twinkling of an eye" and the earth will be consumed by fire. (D&C 43:32). The wicked shall be cast into unquenchable fire and nobody shall know their fate until they come before Jesus to be judged. Jews that are scattered among the nations will remain until the times of the Gentiles are fulfilled. In that day, the earth will be in great commotion; the love of men will grow cold and selfishness will abound. There will be earthquakes and there will be widespread desolation. Many signs and wonders will appear in the heavens and the earth. The sun will be darkened, the moon will turn to blood, and stars will fall from heaven. Jesus will appear "in the clouds of heaven, clothed with power and great glory" (D&C 45:44). The saints that have died "shall come forth to meet (Jesus) in the cloud" (D&C 45:45).

The wicked will be cast into the fire and the Jews will "lament because they persecuted their king" (D&C 45:53). The heathen nations shall be redeemed and "shall have part in the first resurrection; and it shall be tolerable for them" (D&C 45:54). Believers who are alive will receive the earth as an inheritance "and their children will grow up without sin unto salvation" (D&C 45:58). Jesus will reign in their midst and he will be their king and lawgiver.

The Lord commands that his people assemble and go forth into the western parts of America. They are to build up churches and a "New Jerusalem, a land of peace, a city of refuge, a place of safety for the saints of the Most High God" (D&C 45:64–66). The glory of the Lord will be there and no wicked people will come into the land and city called Zion.

Elders are to conduct church meetings "as they are directed and guided by the Holy Spirit" (D&C 46:2). Everyone is welcome to attend public meetings. Church members and those "earnestly seeking the kingdom" are not to be excluded from "sacrament meetings" unless they have sinned (D&C 46:4–5). In this case, members may be admitted after making reconciliation. Every believer in Jesus has a least one gift bestowed by the Holy Ghost. Some of the gifts are administration, diversity of operations, wisdom, knowledge, healing, miracles, prophecy, discerning of spirits, tongues, and interpretations of tongues.

Those who receive Jesus shall be saved but those who do not shall be dammed. All men must repent for all are under sin, except those who God has reserved as holy men (D&C 49:8). The requirements for salvation are faith in Jesus, repentance, baptism and the gift of the Holy Ghost "by the laying on of the hands of the elders of the church" (D&C 49:14). Those who forbid marriage are not following God "for marriage is ordained by God unto man" (D&C 49:15). Likewise, those who forbid eating meat are not following God. The saints will not be saved unless they take up their crosses and keep God's commandments (D&C 56:2).

The land of Missouri is the land of inheritance where the City of Zion is to be built. The center of the Promised Land is Independence, Missouri. This is where the temple is to be built. The disciples are to purchase land so that it can become "an everlasting inheritance" (D&C 57:5). The saints are to be subject to the laws of the land. Disciples are to contribute money to the bishop to purchase land for the storehouse and house of printing in Independence, Missouri. The disciples are to "open their hearts" and "purchase this whole region of country as soon as time will permit" (D&C 58:52).

Those who are faithful to do good works, obey God's commands, and build up the land of Zion shall be blessed both spiritually and materially. Members are to love God with all their might, mind, and strength. They are to rest from their labors and gather to "offer up sacraments upon my holy day" (D&C 59:9). Those that do works of righteousness will be rewarded with peace in this world and eternal life (D&C 59:23). The elders are to travel two by two and preach the gospel "among the congregations of the wicked" (D&C 60:8, 13–14).

Those who look at a woman to lust after her or commit adultery in their hearts do not have the Spirit and have denied the faith (D&C 63:16). All those who are unbelievers, liars, whoremongers, and sorcerers shall burn in the lake of fire. Those who endure in faith and obey God's commandments shall receive an inheritance upon the earth when the day of transfiguration comes. Those who die and are faithful will rise from the dead and "receive an inheritance before the Lord in the holy city" (D&C 63:49). Those who are faithful and alive shall grow old and die but "they shall not sleep in the dust, but they shall be changed in the twinkling of an eye" (D&C 63:51). When Jesus returns to the earth, the angels shall separate the wicked from the righteous and cast the wicked into the lake of fire.

Those who tithe shall not be burned at the return of Jesus to the earth (D&C 64:23). The words spoken by elders "when moved by the Holy Ghost shall be scripture" (D&C 68:4). These words represent the will, mind, and voice of the Lord. Those who believe the gospel and are baptized will be saved but those who do not shall be dammed.

High priests shall be appointed by the First Presidency of the Melchizedek Priesthood except for those who are "literal descendants of Aaron" (D&C 68:15). In order to be considered, candidates must prove their lineage or have it ascertained by revelation from the Lord under the hands of the First Presidency. No high priest or bishop "shall be tried or condemned for any crime, save it be before the First Presidency of the church" (D&C 68:22).

Parents are to teach their children "the doctrine of repentance, faith in Christ the Son of the Living God, and of baptism and the gift of the Holy Ghost by the laying on of the hands, when eight years old" (D&C 68:25). Parents sin unless they teach their children these things. Children of members shall be baptized when they are eight years old and receive the laying on of hands.

Elders are to "render an account of their stewardship" to their bishop who, in turn, must report to the "bishop in Zion" (D&C 72:5-6). Elders who remain faithful in preaching the gospel will gain eternal life. Believers should not marry or remain married to an unbeliever unless the religious ordinances of the unbeliever, such as circumcision of male children, are not followed. Religious ordinances such as circumcision and baptism that are required because children are unholy are wrong. Little children are holy because they are sanctified through the atonement of Jesus Christ (D&C 74:5-7).

Those who deny the truth and defy the Lord are "sons of perdition" and are "doomed to suffer the wrath of God, with the devil and his angels in eternity" (D&C 76:32-33). These sons of perdition are those who deny the Holy Spirit and "the Only Begotten Son of the Father" (D&C 76:35). They are the only ones "who shall not be redeemed but they shall go away into everlasting punishment" (D&C 76:36-38).

In contrast, those of the church of the Firstborn: 1) believe in Jesus; 2) are baptized being buried in water in his name; 3) keep the commandments; 4) receive the Holy Spirit by the laying on of hands by an ordained elder and 5) overcome by faith and are "sealed by the Holy Spirit" (D&C 76:51-53). These Firstborn of the church are "priests of the Most High, after the order of Melchizedek" and are "gods, even the sons of God" (D&C 76:57-58). They shall dwell in the presence of God and his Christ forever and they shall accompany Jesus when he comes "in the clouds of heaven to reign on earth over his people" (D&C 76:63). These blessed people shall partake of the first resurrection and have celestial bodies "whose glory is like that of the sun" (D&C 76:70).

There is a second group of redeemed people called Terrestrial. These people have less glory than those of the Church of the Firstborn. They include those who died ignorant of God's commandments but received the testimony of Jesus as spirits while they were in prison where Jesus preached the gospel to them. They are honorable people who were blinded by the craftiness of men. They "receive the presence of the Son but not the fullness of the Father" (D&C 76:75–77).

A third group of redeemed people is called Telestial. Their glory is less than those of the Terrestrial are. These people did not receive the gospel of Christ, did not deny the Holy Spirit, and were "thrust down to hell" (D&C 76:82–84). They "shall not be redeemed from the devil until the last resurrection" (D&C 76:85). These people are "liars, sorcerers, adulterers, whoremongers and "suffer the wrath of God on earth" and "the vengeance of eternal fire" (D&C 76:104–105). The inhabitants of the Telestial world are "as innumerable as the stars in the firmament of heaven, or as the sand upon the seashore" (D&C 76:109). They "shall be servants of the Most High; but where God and Christ dwell they cannot come, worlds without end" (D&C 76:112). Ahman is another name for Jesus (D&C 78:20).

Members of the church in good standing are to be provided for by the church if they are widows, orphans or poor (D&C 83:6).

In 1832 Joseph Smith received a revelation in which he said the New Jerusalem is to be built in a spot "appointed by the finger of the Lord, in the western boundaries of the State of Missouri, and dedicated by the hand of Joseph Smith Jun., and others with whom the Lord was well pleased" (D&C 84:3). A temple is to be built and the "cloud of the Lord shall rest upon it" and fill it (D&C 84:5).

Abraham received the priesthood from Melchizedek who received it through the lineage of his fathers, even until Adam (D&C 84:14–16). This priesthood continues "in the church of God in all generations, and is without beginning of days or end of years" (D&C 84:17). Another lower priesthood was conferred on Aaron and his seed throughout all their generations. The greater priesthood of Melchizedek, which ended with Moses, has the "key of the mysteries of the kingdom, even the key of the knowledge of God" (D&C 84:19). However, the Israelites failed to keep the ordinances necessary to "behold the face of God" (D&C 84:23). Therefore, Moses and the Holy Priesthood were removed from them but the lesser priesthood of Aaron remained. The gospel of this lesser priesthood is based on repentance, baptism remission of sins, the law, and "carnal commandments" (D&C 84:27). The offices of bishop and elder are appendages of the higher priesthood of Moses while the offices of teacher and deacon are appendages of the lesser priesthood of Aaron. High priests, elders and lesser priests are to travel and proclaim the gospel but "deacons and teachers should be appointed to watch over the church" (D&C 84:111). Men remain under condemnation unless they repent and embrace the new covenant which is the Book of Mormon and follow God's commandments (D&C 84:57).

In 1832, Joseph Smith predicted that war would "shortly come to pass, beginning at the rebellion of South Carolina" (D&C 87:1). The Southern States will be "divided against the Northern States" and they will seek help from Great Britain and the other nations (D&C 87:1). The people of the earth will mourn and suffer famine, plagues, and earthquakes. The people of the earth will "feel the wrath and indignation from and the chastening hand of an Almighty God, until the consumption decreed hath made a full end of all nations" (D&C 87:6).

Those who keep God's laws shall be resurrected and crowned with glory in the presence of God the Father. They shall possess the Celestial kingdom. Those who are not "sanctified through the law I have given unto you, even the law of Christ, shall inherit a lesser Terrestrial or Telestial kingdom" (D&C 88:21).

The gospel shall go forth and be followed by earthquakes, thunder, tempests, and great fear and commotion among mankind. Angels shall fly through the heavens shouting: "Prepare ye, prepare ye O inhabitants of the earth; for the judgment of our God is come" (D&C 88:92). A sign shall appear in heaven that shall be seen by all people. The saints that are alive upon the earth shall be quickened and caught up to meet Jesus. Those saints who have "slept in their graves" shall come forth and also meet Jesus in the air (D&C 88:96–97).

A second angel shall call to resurrection those who have died and whose spirits subsequently received the gospel of Jesus. A third angel then announces to the rest of the dead who are under condemnation that they will not be raised for another thousand years which is the end of the earth (D&C 88:99–101).

A fourth angel announces to those who are found to remain in their sins without any future redemption. A fifth angel says that everyone shall give glory to God for the time of judgment is come. A sixth angel announces the fall of Babylon. A seventh angel says, "It is finished! The Lamb of God hath overcome" and has trodden the winepress of God's wrath (D&C 88:106). Each of the seven angels in turn announces the mighty works of God and the acts of men during each thousand-year period. The seventh angel announces that there shall no longer be any more time and that Satan shall be bound for a thousand years. Then Satan shall be loosed for a short time and shall gather his armies and fight Michael, who is the seventh angel, and the hosts of heaven. The devil and his armies shall be cast away into their own place and shall not have power over the saints anymore (D&C 88:110–114).

Joseph Smith says that strong drinks "are not for the belly but for the washing of your bodies" (D&C 89:7). Likewise, "tobacco is not for the body, neither for the belly" but is to be used as an herb for "bruises and sick cattle" (D&C 89:8). Hot drinks are also forbidden but "all grain is good for the food of men" (D&C 89:14). The flesh of animals may be eaten but only sparingly.

Joseph Smith, Sidney Rigdon, and Frederick Williams all hold the keys of the last kingdom of God. These keys will never be taken away. The Old Testament Apocrypha are not translated as they contain a mixture of things that are and are not true.

The world was made by Jesus who is the messenger of salvation, the redeemer of the world and the Spirit of truth (D&C 93:8–10). Those who are faithful and keep the commandments shall partake of the glory of the Lord and are the Church of the Firstborn (D&C 93:18–22). Mankind also existed "in the beginning with God" as intelligence or the light of truth (D&C 93:29).

Tithes are to be used to build a house, which is to be used by the President of the Church in Zion (Jackson County, Missouri). This house is to be a place of thanksgiving and instruction for those who are called to minister. As long as no unclean thing comes into this house, God's presence will be there "and the pure in heart that shall come into it shall see God" (D&C 97:15-16). The house of the Presidency is to be built with a lower court for preaching, fasting, and praying while the higher court is for a school for the apostles. A second house is to be built next to it and dedicated to printing the translation of Mormon scriptures.

Enemies are to be forgiven if they repent. However, if they refuse to repent after three times and remain steadfast in refusing to make peace, they shall not be forgiven until they repent and pay three times in all things wherein they have trespassed. Enemies who refuse to repent according to this guidance will be punished a hundred times by God (D&C 98:39-44).

The saints suffer persecutions in Missouri, which God says are due to their transgressions. Those who do not endure chastening and deny Jesus will not be sanctified. The saints are not to lose heart but are to press ahead in purchasing land to establish Zion in Missouri for "Zion shall not be moved out of her place" (D&C 101:17). No other place will be appointed until the day comes when there is found no more room for the saints at which time God will appoint other places.

When Jesus returns every corruptible thing including men shall be consumed. The elements shall "melt with fervent heat; and all things shall become new" (D&C 101:25). The enmity of men, beasts, and all flesh shall cease. Satan shall have no power to tempt men. There will be no longer any sorrow for there is no more death. Infants will grow to be "as old as a tree" and then they will be "changed in the twinkling of an eye" to a glorious rest (D&C 101:30-31).

Church matters and disputes that can't be settled by the church or bishop's council are to be referred to the church high council consisting of twelve high priests and one to three presidents. Church council vacancies are to be filled by nominations from the president(s) that are sanctioned by the high council. Church officers that are faithful will be blessed but those who are not will be cursed. The church shall appoint to each member his or her portion to give to the advance the gospel. Anyone who does not give to the church "his portion, according to the law of my gospel, unto the poor and needy, he shall, with the wicked, lift up his eyes in hell, being in torment" (D&C 104:18). Two church treasuries are to be established. One is for sacred things that are to be kept in a sealed place. None of these sacred things can be taken out except "by the voice of the order, or by commandment" (D&C 104:64). The second treasury is for all the income obtained by the members as soon as it is received (D&C 104:68). All income from properties or livestock given to members from church resources shall be immediately placed into the church treasury.

There are two priesthoods in the church: the Aaronic (which is the lesser and includes the Levitical Priesthood)[40] and the Melchizedek Priesthood (which is called the Holy Priesthood after the Order of the Son of God prior to Melchizedek). The president, high priests, and elders are under the Melchizedek Priesthood. The president and high priests have authority to act as any other officer of the church such as bishop, Levitical priest, teacher, and deacon. There is a president and council over every office of the church but they are under the authority of the Office of the High Priesthood. The bishop is the highest office of the Aaronic Priesthood, which is conferred based on lineage from Aaron or appointment by revelation.

The Aaronic Priests "hold the keys of the ministering of angels and to administer outward ordinances" such as baptism (D&C 107:20). There are twelve apostles and the seventy called to preach the gospel. These two groups form two quorums or

---

40   The Levitical Priesthood is rarely used in the LDS Church.

decision-making bodies. The twelve are a traveling and presiding high council to regulate the affairs of the church in all nations. The seventy act under the direction of the twelve and the high council at Zion. The seventy assist in the preaching and administering the gospel as needed. The twelve ordain ministers "designated unto them by revelation" (D&C 107:39). The President of the High Priesthood presides over the entire church and is a "seer, revelator, a translator, and a prophet, having all the gifts of God which he bestows upon the head of the church" (D&C 107:91–92).

Adam bestows his last blessing upon the righteous residue of his sons and he ordains them in the Valley of Adam-ondi-Ahman. The Lord appears to them and blesses Adam naming him Michael the Archangel.

Moses appears to Joseph Smith and Oliver Cowdery and gives them the keys of the gathering of Israel from the four parts of the earth. Next Elias appears and grants them the "gospel of Abraham" saying that through them and their descendants all the nations will be blessed (D&C 110:12). Finally, Elijah appears and delivers "the keys of this dispensation" by which "ye may know that the great and dreadful day of the Lord is near" (D&C 110:16). In the last days, the church will be called The Church of Latter-day Saints. Spring Hill in Davis County, Missouri is the place where "Adam shall come to visit his people or the Ancient of Days shall sit" (D&C 116:1).

The Lord requires that members give all their surplus property to the church plus one-tenth of their interest income annually.[41] Almost all men are by nature disposed to exercise unrighteous dominion over others as soon as they get a little authority. Joseph Smith urges members to missionary work for there are "sects, parties and denominations who are blinded by

---

41   Not so at present. This is The Law of Consecration in its fullness, which was given initially to leading elders, but many did not keep it so the Law of Tithing was given to the Church.

the subtle craftiness of men" and who are kept from the truth because they don't know where to look for it (D&C 123:12–13).

Baptisms for the dead are to be performed in temples. Stock is issued to members of the church in order to build a boarding house in Nauvoo, Illinois. Hyrum is to take the office of Priesthood and Patriarch appointed to him by his father. Hyrum has the keys of binding and loosing, blessing and cursing on earth and in heaven.

Hyrum becomes a prophet, seer, and revelator the same as Joseph Smith. A recorder and three witnesses are to bear witness to baptisms for the dead so that proper certifications are recorded. In this way, the salvation of the dead who have died without knowledge of the gospel is attained through the binding and loosing authority of the church (D&C 128:8). Because the church has binding and loosing authority, the dead shall be credited the ordinance of baptism and their names recorded in the Book of Life in heaven if they receive it. God has given this ordinance to the church for the salvation of those whose agents shall properly follow this doctrine. The salvation and perfection of the living and the dead depend on each other (D&C 128:15; 18).

There are two kinds of beings in heaven: angels, who are resurrected people with bodies of flesh and bones and spirits of just men without resurrected bodies. Evil spirits, such as the devil, do not have flesh and bones and can be discerned because they will offer you their hand to shake if you ask. Righteous spirits will not offer to shake hands when asked because they will not attempt to deceive. In this way, good and evil spirits and angels can be discerned (D&C 129:1–8).

Joseph says that John 14:23 refers to a personal appearance of the Father and Son. "The idea that the Father and Son dwell in a man's heart is an old sectarian notion and is false" (D&C 130:3). The only angels are those who belong or have belonged to the earth. Angels reside in "the presence of God, on a globe like a sea of glass and fire" (D&C 130:7).

The place where God resides is a great Urim and Thummim. The earth will be remade into a crystal and will be an Urim and Thummim to all who dwell on it. The white stone mentioned in Revelation 2:17 will become an Urim and Thummim to each individual who receives one. Things of a higher order of kingdoms will be revealed to those who are given such a white stone (D&C 130:8–10). Those who have more knowledge and intelligence in this life will retain this advantage in the world to come. The Father and Son each have a body "of flesh and bones tangible as a man's but the Holy Spirit "has not a body of flesh and bones but is a personage of spirit. Were it not so, the Holy Ghost could not dwell in us" (D&C 130:22).

There are three heavens or degrees of celestial glory. Only those who are married in the church can attain the highest celestial heaven. "There is no such thing as immaterial matter. All spirit is matter but it is more fine or pure, and can only be discerned by pure eyes" (D&C 131:7).

A new and everlasting covenant is revealed by Joseph Smith. Those who do not keep this covenant are dammed "for no one can reject this covenant and be permitted to enter into my glory" (D&C 132:4). Joseph Smith holds the power of God's new and everlasting covenant. "There is never but one on the earth at a time on whom this power and keys to this priesthood are conferred" (D&C 132:7).

Those married outside the church are not bound by any law after death. They are appointed to be angels and serve those "who are worthy of a far more, and an exceeding and eternal weight of glory" (D&C 132:15–16). These people remain angels and do not become gods but minister to those who attain godhood (D&C 131:4; 132:17). Those married by an anointed and appointed minister of the LDS Church are joined by the Lord in an eternal covenant and shall become gods and "inherit thrones, kingdoms, principalities, powers, dominions and all heights and depths" (D&C 132:19). Only couples thus married can attain this glory. However, such couples must also obey God's laws and follow the narrow way that leads to such exultation (D&C 132:21). Relatively few attain godhood since most do not know Jesus and this new covenant. "Broad is the gate and wide the way that leadeth to the deaths; and many there are that go in thereat, because they receive me not, neither do they abide in my law" (D&C 132:25).

Those who commit murder shedding innocent blood and reject the new covenant after having received it are dammed. Such people have committed an unforgivable sin and shall never enter into God's glory (D&C 132:27).

Joseph Smith is granted the power to forgive sins. A woman whose husband has committed adultery can be given to another faithful man through the authority of the Holy Priesthood (D&C 132:44). If any man of the church marries a virgin and wishes to marry another virgin, he may do so with the permission of his first wife. Such men may have more than one wife without committing adultery. Those who break their marriage vows commit adultery and shall be destroyed (D&C 132:61–63).

Jesus shall return to the New Jerusalem and the righteous dead will be resurrected. Those who repent and sanctify themselves will be given eternal life. Those who reject God's servants and laws will be delivered into darkness where there is "weeping and wailing, and gnashing of teeth" (D&C 133:73).

Governments are instituted by God for the benefit of man. Laws must protect freedom of conscience, the right to own property and protect life for there to be peace. Laws must be enforced equally and justly. Government does not have the right to infringe on religious practices such as how to worship and public or private devotions. Men are bound to "sustain and uphold the respective governments in which they reside, while protected in their inherent and inalienable rights by the laws of such governments" (D&C 134:5). No religious society has the right to take life or property or to inflict physical punishment on their members. "They can only excommunicate them from their society and withdraw from them fellowship" (D&C 134:10). Civil authorities should deal with infringements of rights, property, or character. However, men may defend themselves from unlawful attacks where immediate appeal to civil authorities is not possible. It is not just to mingle religious influence with civil government whereby one form is favored and given privileges that others are denied.

The gospel is to be proclaimed throughout the earth except to those slaves whose masters object. There is to be no meddling with slaves to influence them "to be dissatisfied with their situations in this life, thereby jeopardizing the lives of men; such influence we believe to be unlawful and unjust, and dangerous to the peace of every government allowing human beings to be held in servitude" (D&C 134:12).

On June 27, 1844, Joseph and Hyrum Smith are martyred when shot in a Carthage jail by an armed mob painted black. Joseph Smith has done more than any other person except Jesus Christ to bring salvation to men. Like many of the Lord's anointed prophets, Joseph's mission and message were sealed with his own blood. Joseph and Hyrum were innocent of any crime being confined in jail by the conspiracy of traitors and wicked men (D&C 135:7).

The gate to the Celestial kingdom is like "circling flames of fire" (D&C 137:2). The Father and the Son sit on a blazing throne and the streets are paved with gold" (D&C 137:3-4). All who have died without knowledge of this gospel but who would have received it if they had been permitted to tarry, shall be heirs of the Celestial kingdom" (D&C 137:7). God judges the works of men according to the desires of their hearts. Therefore, he admits those who "would have received it (the gospel) with all their hearts" if they would have had the opportunity during their lives (D&C 137:8). Children who die before the age of accountability "are saved in the Celestial kingdom of heaven" (D&C 137:10).

Mankind is saved by the atonement of Jesus and by obedience to the principles of the gospel" (D&C 138:4). According to Joseph Smith, the third and fourth chapters of the book of first Peter describe the descent of Jesus to a prison where the spirits of the righteous dead are assembled to await their resurrection from the bonds of death. Jesus organizes and sends the righteous spirits to go and carry the gospel to those that are in darkness even to all the spirits of men. In this way, the gospel was preached "to those who had died in their sins without knowledge of the truth or in transgression having rejected the prophets" (D&C 138:32).

Joseph and Hyrum Smith, Brigham Young, John Taylor, William Woodruff "and other choice spirits" are among the "noble and great ones who were chosen in the beginning to be rulers in the Church of God (D&C 138:53). Even before they were born, they, with many others, received their first lessons in the world of spirits and were prepared to come forth in the due time of the Lord to labor in his vineyard for the salvation of the souls of men" (D&C 138:56). Faithful elders of the Church of the Latter-day Saints continue as spirits after death to proclaim the gospel of repentance and redemption through the sacrifice of the Only Begotten Son. They go to those to those who are in the darkness and bondage of sin in the world of the spirits of the dead. The dead spirits who repent are redeemed and shall receive a reward according to their deeds. However, they must first pay the penalty of their sins and be washed clean before they become heirs of salvation (D&C 138:57–59).

In 1890, Wilford Woodruff, who was the President of the Church of Jesus Christ of Latter-day Saints, wrote an official declaration in which he denied the teaching of polygamy or its practice in the church. The Church is directed to submit to the governing laws of the country that forbid polygamy. Any elder of the Church who teaches polygamy is to be reproved. In 1978, Eldon Tanner First Counselor in the First Presidency of the Church presented a declaration in which "all of the blessings and privileges and blessing which the gospel affords" were extended to worthy members (OD 2). Worthy male members became eligible to be ordained to the priesthood without regard of race or color.

AUTHOR COMMENTS ─────────────────────────────

Joseph Smith and Oliver Cowdery translate a version of a parchment written by the Beloved Apostle John using the Urim and Thummim. Jesus tells John that he will not die until he returns. John is to be "a flaming fire and a ministering angel to those who will become heirs of salvation" (D&C 7:6). In John 21:20–24, Peter asks Jesus to reveal what will happen to John. Jesus replies, "If I want him to remain alive until I return, what is that to you?" Because of this statement, a rumor spread among believers that John would not die but Jesus did not say that he would not die. John clarifies that Jesus did not say that he would live until the return of Jesus. Therefore, the translation by Joseph Smith and Oliver Cowdery conflicts with the Bible. There is no historical or other evidence that John is presently alive and ministering to those who believe or will believe in Jesus.[42]

In *Doctrines and Covenants* 11:30, Jesus says, "as many as receive me, to them will I give power to become the sons of God, even to those who believe in my name." This verse is similar to John 1:12. Both these verses say that salvation is based on faith in Jesus and receiving him as personal savior and Lord. However, there are many verses in the Mormon books of scripture that say that faith plus church ordinances, or works and keeping the laws of God are required for salvation. Refer to Table 1 for a list of some examples.

D&C 49:8 says that all men are under sin and must repent except for some holy men that are known to God alone. This implies that not all men are sinful and in need of a savoir, which contradicts what the Bible says (Rom 3:23).

Joseph Smith and Oliver Cowdery are visited by an angel who is John the Baptist. This angel bestows the Priesthood of Aaron, which involves the ministry of angels, gospel of repentance and baptism by immersion for the remission of sins. There is no basis

─────────────────────

42   A rather fallible foundation to build a spiritual argument.

in the Bible to support the view that saints whose bodies are resurrected become angels.[43] Angels are mentioned at least 108 times in the Old Testament and 165 times in the New Testament without any mention of them being dead people. There is one case where the spirit of a dead person appears among the living. This is recorded in 1 Samuel 22:12–15 where the witch of Endor conjures the spirit of Samuel from the grave. It is debatable whether the spirit that appeared really was Samuel or a demon in disguise, but what is clear is that this spirit was not referred to as an angel and did not have a body.

There are different ranks and types of angels such as cherubs and seraphs that have wings and many eyes suggesting that these creatures are different from humans (2 Kgs 19:15; Isa 6:1–3).[44] The spirits of Moses and Elijah appeared with Jesus at his transfiguration and are described as men in glorious splendor, not as angels (Luke 9:30–31). Angels can appear as humans as is seen in the story of Sodom and Gomorrah (Gen 19:1–12). In conclusion, while there is evidence that angels appear as humans, there is no evidence to suggest that humans become angels.

According to *Doctrines and Covenants* 27:11, Adam is Michael the Archangel. This appears to conflict with the statement in D&C 29:36 that says "the devil was before Adam." If the devil is a fallen angel and angels are humans in resurrected bodies, then how can the devil exist before Adam? According to the LDS view, the devil (Lucifer) and Michael (pre-mortal Adam) were both before Adam the mortal man. While I understand the LDS view of pre-mortal spirits becoming human, the point remains that the Mormon scriptures refer to these entities as angels and defines angels as humans with resurrected bodies. Thus, the apparent contradiction remains.

---

43   Hence the need for a second clarifying witness.

44   All symbolic and not literal. Angels are always people, both pre-mortal and post-mortal and symbolically speaking even mortals for does not God perform miracles through each other?

In addition, the Bible says that the devil or Satan was formerly known as Lucifer prior to being cast down to the earth (Is 14:12–14). The Bible says that the devil was cast down to the earth by Michael the Archangel (Rev 12:7). According to D&C 27:11 & 107:54, Adam is Michael the Archangel. One view of this passage is that it refers to the final removal of the devil from heaven and so it refers only to a future event. However, Lucifer was called the devil in the book of Genesis so he must have at least lost his position as covering cherub prior to the fall of man. Since the fall of Adam, the devil roams the earth but still has access to the throne of God (Job 1:6–7). Michael is the angel who argues with the devil over the body of Moses (Joel 1:9). According to D&C 129:1, angels are resurrected people and have bodies of flesh and bones. If Adam becomes Michael the Archangel after he dies and is resurrected, he cannot be the angel who confronts the devil over the body of Moses after he dies (Jude 9) since he has not yet been resurrected. In addition, Michael appears to be a pre-eminent angel and the nemesis of Satan who is able to successfully argue and fight with him. If Michael did not cast Lucifer down to the earth prior to the fall of man, who did?

According to LDS teaching, Satan rebelled and was cast out of heaven with a third of the heavenly spirit children because God chose Jesus to redeem mankind. This resulted in the denial of further development for Satan and his followers.[45] Since Satan and his followers were spirit children when they were cast from heaven, they cannot have physical bodies and do not qualify as angels. Finally, in Revelation 7:9–12, angels and men are spoken of as two separate groups of creatures who have different songs to sing as they worship God.

Those who kill commit a sin that can never be pardoned and so they are condemned to hell (D&C 42:18). The Bible speaks of an unpardonable sin but it is blasphemy or rejection of the Holy

---

45   *Gospel Principles* (2009), 16.

Spirit (Matt 12:31–32). There is no evidence in the Bible to support the view that there is more than one unpardonable sin and that it is murder. Jesus said that anyone who is angry with his brother is in danger of committing murder in thought, which is a sin (Matt 5:21–22). Indeed anyone who hates his brother sins and is under judgment without the atoning blood of Jesus (1 Jn 3:15). Thus, if killing is the unpardonable sin, then nobody can be forgiven since everyone becomes angry with others and wishes evil or thinks ill of them.[46] D&C 42:18 says, "Thou shalt not kill; and he that kills shall not have forgiveness in this world, nor in the world to come." While I understand the Mormon view that some will suffer in hell for a season and then go to a heavenly kingdom, in order to accept this Mormon view, one has to ignore the clear meaning of these words.

D&C 59:23 teaches that those who do works of righteousness will be rewarded in this life with blessings and peace as well as with eternal life after death. This appears to be a form of the popular prosperity gospel preached today that God wants believers to be healthy, wealthy and enjoy the best of this world and the world to come. This contrasts with the words of Jesus who warned that those who believe in him will find conflict with loved ones (John 10:34–36). Jesus says that his followers will be persecuted and that those who would follow him must deny themselves for the sake of Christ which are clearly at odds with the prosperity gospel (John 10:38–39).

According to D&C 68:9, those who believe in Jesus and are baptized will be saved but those who do not believe will be dammed. The Mormon concept of damnation differs from the rest of Christianity in that it can be eternal or temporary. Only those who persistently reject Jesus and the promptings of the Holy

---

46 Mormons believe just as the Bible regarding the unpardonable sin. When D&C 42:18 refers to "no forgiveness," that refers to murder precluding an individual from the Celestial Kingdom. After a time in hell, even murderers will go to the Telestial Kingdom.

Ghost remain in hell for eternity and are called sons of perdition. Others may hear the gospel while in hell (preached by select Mormon elders) and be released after suffering for their sins for a time into the Terrestrial kingdom.

Mormon holy scriptures can continue to expand as ordained elders speak as they are moved by the Holy Ghost (D&C 68:4). As recently as 1995, the president of the Church of Jesus Christ of Latter Day Saints (LDS) received a revelation that was accepted as scripture.[47] The Bible is the story of the creation, rebellion, redemption, and restoration of mankind and creation. Major Christian denominations (except for LDS) believe that the last of the holy books were written in the 1st century AD by the apostles or those who were their disciples and therefore, no more holy scriptures will be revealed. The New Testament book of Revelation is the last book written and it completes the story of events to come culminating with the final judgments of the devil and those who follow him, the blessings of those who have faith in Jesus and the creation of a new heaven and earth.

The book of Revelation concludes with a statement that it is the end of God's scriptures. A curse is pronounced upon any who add or subtract from it:

> I warn everyone who hears the words of the prophecy of this book: If anyone adds anything to them, God will add to him the plagues described in this book. And if anyone takes words away from this book of prophecy, God will take away from him his share in the tree of life and in the holy city, which are described in this book. (Rev 22:18-19).

A view consistent with Mormonism is that this curse only applies to the Book of Revelation and it does not mean that no

---

47   The Proclamation to the World on the Family

further scriptures are to be given by God. Most of the scriptures in the *Book of Mormon* were written before the birth of Jesus. The Mormon books of Fourth Nephi, Mormon, Ether, and Moroni detail events after the Book of Revelation was written. However, the holy scriptures of Mormonism include the Doctrines and Covenants and The Pearl of Great Price, which are based on revelations or translations of the Bible by Joseph Smith and other LDS leaders. Parts of these books describe future events such as the final judgment of the wicked and the new heaven and earth. While there are similarities in these books to Revelation, there are also unique predictions and an expansion of concepts described in Revelation. An example is the idea that the wicked and those who die without faith in Jesus will be given a second chance to believe as the spirits of the righteous dead preach the gospel to them. The concepts of the Celestial, Terrestrial, and Telestial kingdoms of God are also not found in the Bible.[48] These ideas describe the fate of mankind and the eternal state of the new heaven and earth. Therefore, these concepts represent additions to the content of Revelation that were written in the 19th century. These concepts clearly fall within the scope of the warning mentioned in Revelation. The Bible says that the gospel was delivered once and for all time to the saints and so there is no continuing revelation as the LDS teaches (Jude 1: 3-4).

People who deny Jesus and the Holy Spirit are the only ones who will be punished forever in the lake of fire with the devil and his angels. (D&C 76:31-36). Some others suffer in the lake of fire temporarily, but are brought out when the dead are resurrected. (D&C 76:38-39). Therefore, most men will be saved, as only those who reject Jesus will suffer the eternal wrath of God. This teaching is contradictory to that of Jesus who said in Matthew 7:13 that most people will be lost and relatively few will enter the narrow gate (i.e., faith in Jesus) that leads to eternal life. Jesus also said

---

48   1 Corinthians 15:40-41

that many are called but few are chosen to become children of God and heirs of eternal life (Matt 22:14). There is no support in the Bible for the idea that some people suffer temporarily in the lake of fire before they are rescued and resurrected into the kingdom of God.

Those people who have Telestial glory are the wicked who are cast down to hell until Jesus returns in glory to the earth. These people are as innumerable as the stars and they shall be servants of God. They are brought out of hell during the second resurrection but they can't dwell with God or Jesus. Their glory is lesser than those who inhabit the Terrestrial kingdom. The idea that there are three distinct kingdoms of God is not found in the Bible. The Bible teaches that men are sent to heaven or hell after death and there are no second chances after death to leave hell for heaven (Heb 9:27; Luke 16:25–26). Both the Bible and the books of Mormonism teach that men shall be rewarded according to their works while alive. These differences in rewards are referred to as places or mansions and not as various worlds or kingdoms (John 14:1–3; D&C 76:111). Finally, D&C 76:103–105 says that wicked people such as sorcerers and adulterers shall suffer the wrath of God in eternal fire. These people will be delivered by Jesus and shall dwell in the Telestial kingdom of God. In contrast, the Bible teaches that adulterers and sorcerers will suffer eternally in the lake of fire. (Rev 21:8).[49]

In 1832, Joseph Smith received a prophecy that the New Jerusalem and temple will be built in Missouri. According to this prophecy, the hand of Joseph Smith will dedicate this city and temple. Since Joseph Smith died before the New Jerusalem was built in Missouri, this verse must mean that the resurrected Joseph Smith will perform this dedication (D&C 84:3-5).

D&C 88:110 says that there will be no more time following the

---

49 Hence the need for ongoing clarifying revelation especially in light of the "Plain and Precious" parts of the Bible that have been lost.

declaration of the seventh angel at the return of Christ and the first resurrection. However, this verse then goes on to say that Satan will be bound for a thousand years.

Enemies are to be forgiven seventy times seven times if they repent and ask forgiveness. However, those who do not repent need only be forgiven up to three times. The fourth time their transgression will not be forgiven until they repent and make four fold reparations for the transgression (D&C 98:39–44).[50] The Bible teaches that we are to love our enemies and forgive them regardless of how many times they sin against us (Matt 5:43–44; 6:14–15).

Proxy baptisms are to be performed in Mormon temples by members and must follow the ordinances of the church. When performed and recorded properly, such baptisms are part of the salvation of those who die ignorant of the gospel. (D&C 128:5). The basis for this is a revelation by Jesus to Joseph Smith wherein he grants the church of LDS the power of priesthood that can lead to the forgiveness of sins such that "whatsoever is bound on earth will be bound in heaven" (D&C 128:8).[51] The idea of binding is said to be equivalent to recording and so baptisms that are properly performed and recorded in Mormon temples on earth result in the forgiveness of the sins of dead people. (D&C 128:8).[52] In contrast, the Bible teaches that salvation results from placing faith in Jesus and is not a result of works such as baptism. (Eph 2:8–9; John 3:16; Rom 10:9–10). At a minimum, the LDS view makes the forgiveness of sins by God contingent on proxy baptisms, which is a work of man.

There are two kinds of creatures in heaven: angels who are resurrected righteous people and the "spirits of just men made

---

50 There is a difference between Church discipline and forgiving others trespasses. This is another paradox of truth: both principles apply.

51 Only God forgives sins. Proxy baptisms can be performed for the deceased that can lead to God's forgiveness.

52 Only if the soul accepts the proxy ordinance, then God can forgive.

perfect" who do not have resurrected bodies but "inherit the same glory" (D&C 129:1–3). Following this line of thinking, there would be no angels in heaven until Jesus ascends to heaven following his death and resurrection. This must be so since Jesus is the firstborn among the dead. (Col 1:18; Rev 1:5). D&C 130:5 says there are no angels in heaven who minister to the earth except those who belong or have belonged to it (i.e., meaning the righteous and resurrected people). This again implies that there are no angels in heaven until after the death and ascension of Jesus. However, angels are mentioned at least 108 times in the Old Testament and appeared on earth as humans with flesh and bones. (Gen 18–19). Furthermore, after the second resurrection, there will be primarily angels in heaven since the bodies of all the righteous people will be resurrected.

The Mormon idea that angels are righteous people with resurrected bodies poses problems with the story of how Joseph Smith received the sacred plates from Moroni. According to the Introduction in the BOM, Moroni appeared to Joseph Smith as a resurrected and glorified being on September 21, 1823. This means that he must have been resurrected between 421–1823AD. However, both the Bible and the BOM teach that the righteous people will not be resurrected until the return of Christ so this is a conflict. This problem has been recognized by some LDS scholars who claim that the spirit of Moroni appeared to Joseph Smith. However, this also poses a problem in how the plates could have been delivered and taken back by a spirit.

Joseph Smith says that the Holy Spirit is a person of spirit and does not have a body and so is unlike the Father and the Son who do have bodies of flesh and bones. (D&C 130:22). He says that this must be so since only the Holy Spirit can indwell believers. This teaching conflicts with various books of the Bible that clearly say that Jesus does indwell believers. An example of this is John 14:20 in which Jesus says that, "I am in the Father, and you are in me and I am in you." This statement only makes sense if the Spirit of God, Jesus, and the Father are a triune God.[53]

In addition, this teaching has serious implications regarding the triune nature of God. If God is three persons in one being, then it does not make sense that the Holy Spirit would lack a physical body. To say that any of the persons of God is not equal to the others in any aspect of being implies inferiority and not equality and unity in essence and being. This teaching by Joseph Smith conflicts with his own teaching in D&C 20:28 which says the "Father, Son and Holy Ghost are one God, infinite and eternal without end." Also, D&C 20:17 says that God is "infinite and eternal, from everlasting to everlasting the same unchangeable God." This appears to be inconsistent with the LDS view that the Holy Ghost does not yet have a body and so one day will experience this change and attain the same state of being as the Father and Son. Finally, Joseph says, "all spirit is matter but it is more fine or pure, and can only be discerned by pure eyes" (D&C 131:7). If this is true, how can the Holy Spirit lack a physical body since spirit is just a pure form of matter?[54]

D&C 131:6 says that it is impossible for people to be saved in a state of ignorance of the gospel. This appears to contradict D&C 137:7–8, which says that some who die without hearing the gospel will still go to the Celestial kingdom. In these cases, God judges that they would have received it if they would have been

---

53　Not to be taken literally. The only literal indwelling is through the spiritual presence of the Holy Spirit. That is His purpose. To impart the Holy Spirit (literally) in terms of His power to infiltrate (when invited/allowed) our minds and hearts through our spirit. Since the Father, Son, and Holy Ghost are one in purpose, the influence of the Holy Ghost is commensurate with the influence of the Father and the Son. This is yet another paradox of truth (one but not one at the same time).

54　The spiritual influence of the Holy Ghost is not seen. It is felt. Eventually, the Holy Ghost will obtain a physical body that will be glorified as Christ and His Father. He will be the last of the Father's spiritual children to obtain such. In the meantime, His mission to help all of us make it back goes forward.

given a chance to hear the gospel during their lifetimes. Also, it is the innocence or ignorance of children that enables them to be saved if they die before they are accountable. Therefore, they can't be among the people mentioned in D&C 131:6 without having conflicting teachings (D&C 93:38; Moro 8:8–11).

An LDS man may have more than one wife provided the prior wife gives her consent and the women are all virgins. (D&C 132:61). This teaching conflicts with Jacob 2:24–28 in which God condemns the taking of multiple wives as an abomination. It could be argued that later revelation clarifies and permits polygamy under certain conditions. However, if D&C 132:61 is such clarifying revelation, the subsequent reversal of this teaching in 1890 and 1893 in Declaration 1 by the LDS President does not make sense.[55] The Bible teaches that believers are to obey the laws of their governments except where such laws conflict with Holy Scriptures (Acts 4:19). The President of LDS reverses Mormon Holy Scripture by prohibiting polygamy because it conflicts with the laws of the United States. This ruling appears to place the welfare of the church above divine revelation as the President explains his fears that LDS property would be confiscated and the temples closed if he did not conform to the laws of the country.[56]

D&C 132:7 says that there can be only one revelator on earth at a time "on whom this power and the keys of the priesthood are conferred." The initial LDS revelator was Joseph Smith. However, this contradicts D&C 124:94 where God also appoints Hyrum Smith to be a revelator in addition to Joseph Smith.

---

55   There is no flip-flop here. Just the seemingly arbitrary will of God, which sometimes condemns it. As Isaiah puts it, God's thoughts and ways are higher than ours. He alone perfectly understands truth with all its paradoxes and timing peculiarities.

56   Divine revelation, in this case, willed that the Church survive, that its mission of bringing souls to Christ can move forward and upward.

THE PEARL OF GREAT PRICE
SELECTIONS FROM THE BOOK OF MOSES

God meets Moses on a mountain where he reveals the earth and all mankind to him.[57] God withdraws and Satan demands that Moses worship him. Moses refuses and Satan departs whereupon God returns and the glory of the Lord is upon Moses. God talks to Moses "face to face" and tells him how he created the heavens and the earth in seven days (Moses 1:2). God says that he "created all things spiritually before they were created naturally" (Moses 3:5). Thus, mankind existed as spirits before God gave people flesh and bones. God tells Moses that Satan offered to be God's son and redeem mankind if God would honor him. However, God grants this to Jesus who obeys the Father and gives him the glory. This causes Satan to rebel and results in his being cast down to become the devil (Moses 4:1–4).

Satan tempts Eve and Adam with the forbidden fruit of the tree of knowledge. Adam and Eve sin by eating this forbidden fruit and are cast out of the Garden of Eden. They till the ground, tend flocks, and have children outside of the Garden of Eden. God speaks to them, giving commandments, but they are shut out from his presence. An angel appears to Adam and tells him to offer sacrifices in the name of God's Son; he needs to repent and call on God in the name of his Son. Adam obeys and is filled with

---

57   God in this chapter is the pre-mortal Jesus Christ

the Holy Ghost. God says that those who believe in the Son and repent of their sins will be saved (Moses 5:8–15).

Cain kills Abel because he loves Satan more than God and glories in his wickedness. God places a curse on Cain, who with his family, is shut out from the presence of God. Wickedness spreads among many men despite the preaching of the gospel "from the beginning, being declared by holy angels sent forth from the presence of God, and by his own voice, and by the gift of the Holy Ghost" (Moses 5:58).

Adam begets righteous sons who call upon the name of the Lord. A book of remembrance in the language of Adam is kept and written by those inspired by the Holy Ghost. Their children are taught to read and write in a pure and undefiled language. A genealogy is kept of the children of God.

Enoch preaches that men "must be born again into the kingdom of heaven, of water and of the Spirit and be cleansed by blood" (Moses 6:59). Enoch says that by baptism with water the commandment of God is kept and by the Spirit men are justified and by the blood of Jesus men are sanctified" (Moses 6:60).

God tells Enoch to warn the people to repent and be baptized in the name of the Father, Son, and Holy Ghost. The words of God are spoken through Enoch and are so powerful that the earth trembles and the mountains flee at his command. The enemies of God flee because the fear of God falls upon them. The Lord dwells with his people and they are blessed and flourish. The Lord calls his people Zion because they are of one heart and mind. They live in righteousness and there are no poor people among them. In the days of Enoch, the people of God build a City called Zion or the City of Holiness. In a vision, God shows Enoch that Zion will be taken up into heaven. Representatives of all the descendants of Adam will be taken up into heaven except for the descendants of Cain who are black. (Moses 7:21–22).

God shows Enoch a vision of Noah, Jesus and the final judgment of the wicked. Noah and his sons follow God and are called sons of God. Giants seek to kill Noah but the Lord protects him and God ordains Noah and commands him to preach the gospel as Enoch had done before him. Noah preaches repentance and baptism in the name of Jesus Christ but the children of men do not listen to him. God decides to destroy mankind except for Noah and his family.

AUTHOR COMMENTS

God created the spirits of men and everything else in heaven in a spiritual sense before the earth was made. (Moses 3:7). Since spirit is just a refined state of matter according to D&C 131:7, this statement does not make sense.[58]

The point here is that D&C 131:7 says that spiritual things are the same as matter being a more refined state. God is all knowing and wise. He does not need a blueprint before he begins construction. Indeed if spiritual things are more refined (i.e., purer or better), then it appears that the blueprint is superior to the final product.

There is no support in the Bible for the idea that God created mankind and everything else spiritually before they were created materially. In addition, there is no support for the ideas that the City of Zion was built in the days of Enoch and taken up into heaven. Likewise, it is incredible to think that Enoch and Noah preached repentance and baptism in the name of Jesus Christ and that men must be born again to enter the kingdom of God to mankind before the flood.

Moses 6:55 says that children are conceived in sin. This idea is consistent with the Bible that teaches that men have a sinful nature from conception and are sinful at birth (Ps 51:5). This conflicts with many Mormon scriptures that say that children

---

58 Why not? Everything in this world built by man starts as an idea, then a blueprint before actual construction. Why does it seem nonsensical that God would create things spiritually first?

are not sinful until they reach the age of accountability (D&C 29:46–47; 137:10).

Moses 1:2 says that Moses saw God face to face and "the glory of God was upon Moses; therefore Moses could endure his presence." Moses 1:5 says that no man can behold the glory of God and remain in the flesh on the earth afterwards. However, Moses continued to live afterwards and so this is a contradiction.

THE BOOK OF ABRAHAM

Elkanah the priest of Pharaoh attempts to offer Abraham as a sacrifice to the Egyptian gods. While on the altar, Abraham calls on the Lord who sends an angel to rescue him. God breaks the altar, destroys the statues of the gods, and kills Elkanah. The first government of Egypt was established by Pharaoh, the eldest son of Egyptus who is the daughter of Ham.

The Lord causes a famine in the land of Ur and tells Abraham to go to a land that God will reveal to him. Abraham goes to the land of Canaan with Lot, his wife Sarai, and his father Terah. Abraham and Lot arrive in Canaan but Terah travels part of the way and remains in Haran. God promises to bless those who bless Abraham and curse those who curse him. Famine in the land of Canaan forces Abraham and Lot to go to Egypt. The Lord tells Abraham to say that Sarai is his sister so the Egyptians will not kill him. God gives Abraham the Urim and Thummim in the land of Ur.

Many noble and great spirits of men are with God before the creation of the world.[59] God tells Abraham's spirit that he will be a ruler. The Gods organize and form the heavens and the earth. They form man from the dust of the earth and put his spirit into him and the man became a living soul. (Abr 5:7). After man is created on the sixth day, the Gods say that mankind shall be "very obedient" (Abr 4:31).

---

59   Jeremiah 1:5

AUTHOR COMMENTS

The first government of Egypt was established by Pharaoh, the eldest son of Egyptus, the daughter of Ham. (Abr 1:25). The term "Pharaoh" is a title taken by the kings of Egypt from around 1500 BC until 323 BC. The title means "great house" and was used to describe the palace of the king. The first Egyptian kings ruled from around 3100 to 2686 BC in what is known as the Early Dynastic Period. The first king of Egypt was named Menes or Narmer, not Pharaoh. Thus, the word "Pharaoh" originated as a title not a person's name. In addition, this title did not originate with the first king of Egypt but was first used to refer to the kings about 1600 years later.[60]

Abram goes to Egypt because famine is severe in the land of Canaan. God tells Abram to lie and instruct his wife Sarai to tell the Egyptians that she is his sister so they will not kill him. (Abr 3:22–25). The Bible says that Abram comes up with the idea and tells Sarai to say that she is his sister because he fears the Egyptians will kill him for Sarai is very beautiful (Gen 12:11–13). There is no indication in the Bible account of this story that God tells Abram to lie. In fact, this teaching is contrary to the Bible, which says that God is holy and therefore lies go against his nature.[61]

Abraham 5:7 says that "the Gods formed man from the dust of the ground." This view is consistent with the LDS belief that God is three separate persons. However, this view appears to conflict with D&C 20:17–18, which says that there is one God who is unchanging and who created man. This apparent contradiction could be explained as meaning one God-head consisting of three

---

60   http://en.wikipedia.org/wiki/Pharaoh

61   Yet God commanded Nephi to kill Laban. This is another example of the Paradox of Truth. God is the Word, and to our mortal eyes, His words sometimes seem inconsistent because truth is paradoxical and God represents perfect truth. His will and commands are always right at the times He gives them and the ways He gives them.

persons. This God-head view is stretched even more when applied to D&C 20:28 and Mormon 7:7, which say that the Father, Son, and Holy Ghost are one God, infinite and eternal without end. Also, 3Nephi 9:15 says that Jesus is in the Father and the Father is in him. In Ether 3:14, Jesus says that he is the Father and the Son. These passages and others such as Alma 11:38–39 and Mosiah 15:4 clearly conflict with the LDS view that Jesus is the first-born spirit child of God the Father.

Furthermore, D&C 93:8–11 explicitly says that Jesus alone made the world using similar language found in the Bible regarding the testimony of John the Baptist about Jesus (John 1:1–3).

BYU Egyptologist Michael Rhodes acknowledges that the papyrus fragments purported to be among those from which *The Book of Abraham* was translated date from about 150–220 BC and so could not have been written by Abraham. None of these surviving documents mentions Abraham or can be related to the text of *The Book of Abraham* (Michael D. Rhodes, *Teaching the Book of Abraham Facsimiles,* 116).

Most of the papyri purported to be *The Book of Abraham* have been lost. The portions of the papyri that are available for review do not correspond to Smith's translation but contain Egyptian funeral writings known as *Book of Breathings*. Possible explanations for these discrepancies offered by LDS scholars include:[62]

1. The book was revealed like *The Book of Mormon* and so no physical evidence remains;
2. The text was on the portions of the papyri that are missing;
3. *The Book of Abraham* manuscript was attached to the *Book of Breathings* and has been separated and lost and
4. The current understanding of Egyptian ideograms is different than it was when they were written.

---

62 FAIRwikiportal.TheBookofAbraham.
http://en.fairmormon.org/Book_of_Abraham/Joseph_Smith_Papyri

JOSEPH SMITH—HISTORY

Joseph Smith was born in 1805 in Sharon, Vermont. His family moved to the state of New York when he was ten years old. During this time, there is a great deal of interest in religion and many converts. Some of the members of his family join the Presbyterian faith. Contentions arise among the Presbyterians, Methodists, and Baptists, which confuses Joseph. He studies the Bible and finds clarity in the first chapter and fifth verse of James which says "If any of you lack wisdom, let him ask of God, that giveth to all men liberally, and upbraideth not; and it shall be given him" (James 1:5).

Joseph goes to the woods and prays for wisdom. He is seized by some power that binds his tongue so that he can't speak. Joseph calls on God for help and a pillar of light appears over his head. The light rests on him and he sees two beings "whose brightness and glory defy all description" standing above him in the air. One of the beings points to the other and tells Joseph "This is My Beloved Son, Hear Him!" Joseph asks which of the Christian denominations is correct and which one he should join. He is told that they are all wrong, that their creeds are an abomination, and that he is not to join any denomination. Joseph goes home and, a few days later, he tells a Methodist preacher about his vision. The preacher tells him his vision is of the devil. Religious leaders persecute Joseph but he remains convinced that he has seen a vision from God.

Joseph is rejected by "the religious sects" and he is "left to all kinds of temptations; and mingling with all kinds of society" such that he falls into "many foolish errors." In 1823, Joseph sees a person standing in the air above the floor near his bed while he is praying for forgiveness of his sins and for another vision. This person says that he is a messenger of God called Moroni and that there are hidden golden plates that give an account of the former inhabitants of the Americas. Moroni also tells him that there are two stones in silver bows fastened to a breastplate called the Urim and Thummim.

Joseph goes to the top of a hill near the village of Manchester, New York and finds the golden plates in the place revealed to him by Moroni. The plates are inside of a stone box with the Urim and Thummim. He tries to remove the contents but is forbidden by Moroni who tells him four years must pass before he can remove the contents. Joseph is instructed to return each year on the same day to receive further instructions. Each year Moroni meets Joseph at this location and tells him what the Lord is going to do, and how and in what manner his kingdom is to be conducted in the last days.

Joseph goes to work for Josiah Stoal to search for a silver mine. While thus employed, he meets and marries Emma Hale in 1827. Religious persecutions regarding his visions and opposition from Emma's family to their marriage prompt Joseph and Emma to return to his father's farm. At the appointed time and place, he receives the contents of the box. Persecutions increase and there are many attempts to get the plates from him until he gives them back to Moroni in 1838.

Joseph and Emma return to her father's house where he begins to translate the plates using the Urim and Thummim. A friend named Martin Harris takes copies of the characters from the plates to a Professor Charles Anthon in New York. The professor says that the characters are Egyptian, Chaldaic, Assyrian, and Arabic and that the translations done by Joseph are accurate.

Oliver Cowdery acts as a scribe while Joseph Smith translates the *Book of Mormon* in 1829. They go to the woods to pray and are visited by a messenger from heaven that descends in a cloud of light. The messenger says he is John the Baptist. He confers the Priesthood of Aaron on them, which holds "the keys of the ministering of angels, and of the gospel of repentance, and of the baptism by immersion for the remission of sins" (JS-H 1:69). The power of the laying on of hands to confer the gift of the Holy Ghost is not included in the Aaronic Priesthood. They baptize each other as instructed and then they ordain each other into the Aaronic Priesthood. As soon as they are baptized, the Holy Ghost falls on them and they prophesy many things.

Persecutions by "professors of religion" continue and they are periodically threatened by mobs. The members of Emma's family, (under Divine providence), have a change of heart and become friendly to Joseph and Oliver such that they protect them from the mobs.

AUTHOR COMMENTS

The plates are taken from Joseph by Moroni on May 2, 1838 and are never seen again. Moroni appears to Joseph as a personage that floats above the ground. This suggests that Moroni is a spirit. According to D&C 129:1–9, spirits do not have physical bodies but those righteous people who are resurrected have physical bodies. There is conflicting evidence regarding whether Moroni was resurrected when he took the plates from Joseph Smith. Moroni writes his farewell and says that soon his spirit will "rest in the paradise of God until my spirit and body shall again reunite" at the first resurrection of the righteous (Moroni 10:34). In the Introduction to the *Book of Mormon* it is said that Moroni was a "glorified and resurrected being" when he appeared to Joseph Smith. If Moroni is a spirit being only, how does he take the plates from Joseph since he is a spirit? If he is a "glorified and resurrected being," there are contradictions with the farewell passage in Moroni since the resurrection of the righteous had not yet occurred. In addition, Moroni should be standing and not floating about if he has a resurrected body.

Oliver Cowdery says that John the Baptist confers the Aaronic Priesthood upon Joseph and himself in order that "the Sons of Levi may yet offer an offering unto the Lord in righteousness"(JS-H Oliver Cowdery footnote). Candidates for the Presidency of the Aaronic Priesthood must demonstrate by genealogy that they are descendants of Aaron or Levi unless this is revealed by God to an elder of the church that holds this office (D&C 68:21). No evidence is presented to suggest that Joseph or Oliver are descendants or either Aaron or Levi which is required according to the Bible (Num 16:40).[63]

The LDS practice of conferring the Aaronic Priesthood based on "worthiness" rather than demonstrated genology or divine revelation appears to conflict with the teachings of the Bible and Mormon scriptures until 1978 when President Eldon Tanner declared that the temple blessings and priesthood are to be extended to all worthy members of the Church (OD 2).

---

63   This explicit requirement does not apply to the last dispensation (present era of Christ's Church). The Aaronic Priesthood may be conferred on all boys and men twelve years and older based solely on worthiness.

THE ARTICLES OF FAITH

The beliefs of the Church of Jesus Christ of Latter-day Saints (LDS) are summarized in this book, which is called *The Articles of Faith*. I have presented these beliefs, as well as some from other Mormon books, and compare them to other Christian denominations in the table below. As can be seen from this table, the LDS beliefs agree with many of the concepts of the Apostle's Creed, which forms the core beliefs of Christianity. However, there are also significant differences that result from additional revelations detailed in Mormon scriptures that are not found in the Bible.

Beliefs	*Unique To Mormonism* (Y/N)	*Comments*
We believe in God, the Eternal Father, and in His Son, Jesus Christ, and in the Holy Ghost	Y	God is three distinct persons.
Men are punished for their own sins and not for the sin of Adam	Y	Infants and young children are without sin until they reach the age of reason
Everyone will go to heaven because of the atonement of Christ except those who reject the gospel or commit murder	Y	Murder is an unpardonable sin in that it requires at least temporary punishment in hell. There are three different heavenly kingdoms.

Beliefs	Unique To Mormonism (Y/N)	Comments
Salvation is by faith in Jesus plus works	N	Some Christian denominations teach that the sacraments impart the grace needed to be saved
The ordinances of the church that are necessary for salvation are: faith in Jesus, repentance, baptism by immersion and laying on of hands to receive the gift of the Holy Ghost	Y	Those who attain the Celestial or highest kingdom of heaven do so through the ordinances of the LDS
Those who administer the ordinances and preach must be called by God and ordained	N	Most Christian denominations have ordained priests or ministers
Church leaders consist of apostles, prophets, pastors, teachers, and evangelists	Y	While most of the church offices are found in other Christian churches, the presidency and high priests appear to be unique
Belief in gift of tongues, prophecy, revelation, visions, healing, interpretations of tongues	N	Pentecostal and other charismatic denominations
The Bible is the Word of God as far as it is translated correctly	N	Most Christian denominations agree. What is debated is whether it is infallible and inspired or altered by men.
The Book of Mormon, Doctrines and Covenants and Pearl of Great Price are holy scriptures	Y	Only Mormons accept these books as authoritative

Beliefs	Unique To Mormonism (Y/N)	Comments
Revelations pertaining to the kingdom of God are still being given	Y	Those who say that the Bible is all they need are wrong and under God's judgment (2 Nephi 28:29; 29:10)
The ten tribes of Israel will be restored and the New Jerusalem will be built on the American continent	Y	The return of Jesus and his millennial reign on earth are believed to be in Jerusalem in Palestine not in the Americas.
Christ will return and reign on the earth	N	Most Christians believe this except for Amellenialists who believe that Christ is *presently* reigning through the Church, and that the "1000 years" of Revelation 20:1–6 is a metaphorical reference to the present church age which will culminate in Christ's return
The earth will be renewed to a state like the Garden of Eden	N	A new earth and heaven will be created which will be like the Garden of Eden
Men should be free to worship God according to the dictates of their conscience	N	Most Christians advocate freedom of worship
Believers are to be obedient to their ruling authorities	N	Romans 13:1–5
Virtuous living and endurance in doing good despite temptations are to be encouraged	N	Philip 4:8-9

Beliefs	Unique To Mormonism (Y/N)	Comments
Jesus is born of the virgin Mary, suffered under Pontius Pilate, was crucified, died and rose from the dead. He ascended into heaven and is seated at the right hand of the Father. He will come again to judge the living and the dead.	N	Apostles Creed
There is one holy catholic and apostolic church.	N	The LDS is the true church. Other Christian denominations are an abomination to God. Roman Catholics also believe they are the true church.
Communion of saints, the forgiveness of sins, resurrection of the body and life everlasting	N	Apostles Creed
Baptisms for the dead is part of the salvation of those who die without the gospel	Y	When properly witness and recorded in an LDS temple, the dead can receive the remission of their sins through baptism
Jesus was born of the Virgin Mary through a conceptual act with God the Father	Y	Christians believe that Jesus was conceived spiritually through the power of the Holy Ghost

AUTHOR REFLECTIONS

Who is God? Who am I? What is my purpose? Is there life after death and, if so, what is it like? These questions are answered by religions and result in various views of mankind, the significance of life and our destiny. I have attempted to objectively summarize the books upon which Mormonism is based and compare them with the Bible and historic facts. This has been a journey of discovery for me, as I had never read these books before. I noticed that there is a mixture of verses on salvation by faith and faith plus works in the *Book of Mormon* that gradually trended towards faith plus works prevalent in the Doctrines and Covenants and Pearl of Great Price. Likewise, the works required for salvation grew more complex beginning with repentance and enduring to death in good works to include ordinances such as baptism and receiving the Holy Ghost by the laying on of hands.

Concepts such as the Trinity, heaven, and salvation versus exaltation also diverged from typical Christian definitions. Such trends are either due to progressive revelation (as Mormons believe) or to the collective evolution of thoughts by LDS leaders in the development of a distinct religion. There are occasions where the meaning of words are different from generally held Christian views. One example is "eternal punishment." Most Christians would understand this as meaning suffering in hell for eternity. The Mormon view of this is different, as they believe that most people will not suffer for eternity in hell but many will suffer there until the second resurrection. Also, a name for God is

"Endless" so "eternal punishment" means the punishment given by God and does not refer to the length of time. (D&C 19:10–12)

After I completed my review of the books upon which Mormonism are based, I had some questions related to the interpretation of some passages in these books. Consequently, I sought information on LDS, Mormon beliefs and Brigham Young University web sites as well as asking questions from LDS members. These sources helped me to clarify the essential questions I posed above which are summarized below.

WHO IS GOD?

Any attempt to describe God must acknowledge that there are limitations and mysteries, which cannot be known or described. This is an exercise in which the creature attempts to describe the creator or the infinite. Ultimately, we are left with what God has chosen to reveal about himself, which leads to divergent views based on what sources are considered divine revelation coupled with our interpretations of them. This divergence of views appears to have resulted among those who call themselves Mormons since some Mormons do not consider all of the writings of Joseph Smith to be inspired and part of their holy scriptures. These Mormons point to the words of Joseph Smith in which he said that a person is only a prophet when speaking under the influence of divine revelation.[64] In addition, prophets may not be able to distinguish between their thoughts and those revealed by God.[65]

A divergence in views regarding the nature of God has developed among Mormons based on whether some writings of Joseph Smith known as the King Follett Discourse and Sermon

64   Ari D. Bruening and David L. Paulsen. *The Development of the Mormon Understanding of God: Early Mormon Modalism and Other Myths.* FARMS Review: Vol. 13, No. 2. 109–169.

65   Charles R. Harrell, *This is My Doctrine, The Development of Mormon Theology*, 23.

in the Grove are inspired or were actually given by Joseph Smith since no word-for-word transcription of his remarks remains.

There appears to be unity in the teaching that God is three distinct persons: Father, Son, and Holy Ghost. Although the members of the God-head are distinct, they are united in their thoughts, purpose, knowledge, truth, and power. The Father and the Son have bodies of flesh and bones but the Holy Ghost does not (D&C 130:22). However, beyond this some significant differences occur.

On April 7, 1844, Joseph Smith delivered a discourse known as the King Follett Letter in which he said that God was once "as man now is" and so God had not always been God. He further said that there are many Gods and that men can become Gods. There are an innumerable number of Gods existing "one above another." In June 1844, Joseph Smith presented a supporting discourse known as the Sermon in the Grove. Joseph was killed shortly after this and so he did not have the opportunity to fully explain and clarify them. There is some evidence that Joseph Smith taught these ideas based on their publication in the local newspaper called the Nauvoo Expositor.

This view of God is very different from the Triune belief found in Christian religions. If God the Father was once a man, then there was a time when he was not omnipotent and omniscient. If this is true, then presumably there was another Father God in control. The belief that there are innumerable Gods one above another and humans are spirit children of God the Father with the potential to become Gods are unique to some Mormons. These Mormons believe that Jesus Christ is the first-born spirit child of God the Father. Jesus is the pre-eminent spirit child in that he has more intelligence than the rest of mankind who are also spirit children of God the Father. The Fatherhood of God implies that there is a Heavenly Mother, which the Mormons believe is yet to be revealed.[66]

---

66   The existence of a Heavenly Mother is made explicit in the 1995 Proclamation to the World on the Family. This proclamation states that we are all the spiritual offspring of heavenly parents.

Proponents of this view are themselves split as to whether the Father's mortality was the same as Jesus or like ordinary mankind. Those who hold to the view that the Father's human existence was like that of Jesus seem to view the God-head as eternal and there are no other Gods before or above this God-head. However, this begs the question of why the Father would or needed to experience humanity. The view that the Father was once like ordinary humans infers that there was a progression to the status of Father God that involved human existence. This view presents the possibility of other Father Gods that preceded the God-head we know.

LDS members that do not accept the King Follett or Sermon in the Grove discourses hold to one eternal God-head with three distinct persons that are in perfect unity regarding the attributes, powers and purposes of its members. Thus, this view of the Trinity is one of unity in purpose and will but not substance. "Humans can progress to an exalted state in which they acquire many of the attributes of God, but they will never become equal with the Godhead."[67]

The *Book of Mormon* and other writings of Joseph Smith reflect a monotheistic view of God until around 1839 (Harrell, 118–119). In Alma 11:28–29, Amulek says there is not more than one God in response to Zeezrom's question. There are other passages in the *Book of Mormon* that clearly state that there is one God while listing three persons (2 Ne 31:21; Mosiah 15:1–5; Morm 7:7). Between 1830 and 1841, Joseph Smith began to distinguish among the various persons of God and refer to them as one God-head. In 1841, Joseph taught that God was not three heads with one body but rather three separate bodies (Ehat and Cook, 63). By 1844, Joseph was teaching that there is an infinite number of Gods consisting of Fathers and Sons (and presumably Holy Ghosts) (Ehat and Cook,

67   Ari D. Bruening and David L. Paulsen (2001). The Development of the Mormon Understanding of God: Early Mormon Modalism and Other Myths FARMS Review: Vol. 13, No. 2.(109-169)

380). Current LDS thinking seems to downplay the idea of humans become Gods in the sense of the Father and Son. BYU religion professor Roger Keller said, "there will always be a qualitative difference between the Father, the Son, and us" (Harrell, 154).

God the Father has a tangible flesh and bones body (D&C 130:22). LDS teaches that Jesus is the literal Son of God because his humanity results from a biological relationship with the Father. This presents a problem with the LDS teaching that Mary was a virgin. However, this has been explained by redefining the meaning of "virgin" to mean a woman that has not known a "mortal" man. If this is true, then God the Father practices polygamy since he has fathered spirit children with a heavenly Mother and Jesus through a union with the Virgin Mary.

WHO AM I?

People are eternal beings that have always existed with God as intelligences. "Intelligence" is the essence of our beings and is light or truth that can't be made (D&C 93:29). Humans existed eternally as intelligences before being created as spirit children by a procreative act involving God the Father and a heavenly mother. Each human being is a literal spirit child of heavenly parents. Everyone existed as a spirit child before the world was created but our memories of this life have been hidden or forgotten once we are born as humans. We are created as humans with bodies with free will and knowledge of good and evil for our development or advancement. There are limits to the development of humans as spirits and so the Father created us as creatures of flesh so we could pass tests of obedience. Apparently failing to be obedient is also part of human development since it seems that we are more successful at failing than obeying (Rom 3:20–23).

Those who accept Jesus as their savior and follow his commands and ordinances of the LDS Church enter the Celestial kingdom and dwell with God. These persons can continue to progress and eventually achieve God likeness but not in being. Those who enter the Terrestrial kingdom or the Telestial kingdom cannot progress beyond them. Those of the Terrestrial kingdom will dwell with Jesus but not the Father. Those of the Telestial kingdom do not dwell with either the Father or Son.

WHAT IS MY PURPOSE?

Humans learn what evil is through our ability to choose and with knowledge of the gospel and God's commandments. Jesus died on the cross to make atonement or pay the penalty of the sins of humanity. Therefore, Mormons believe that almost everyone will enter the kingdom of heaven. Only those who blaspheme and reject the Holy Ghost will go to hell for eternity and are called sons of perdition. Sons of perdition are relatively few people. Those who never hear the gospel; are wicked or murder go to hell but not for eternity. Everyone except the sons of perdition will be resurrected to one of the three heavenly kingdoms by the second resurrection. (D&C 76:32–38)

Eternal rewards and places of authority are determined by faith in Jesus Christ, keeping God's commandments and by righteous works. Therefore, Mormons strive to learn and live the commandments of their scriptures and partake of the sacraments of the LDS Church in order to progress in their spiritual development towards godhood.

WHAT IS LIFE LIKE AFTER DEATH?

Mormons believe there are three heavenly kingdoms. Those who repent and place their faith in Jesus Christ as an atoning sacrifice for sins go to the Celestial kingdom after death. They will dwell in the presence of the Father and Son and have glorious bodies that shine like the sun. Mormon families whose parents are sealed in marriage in Mormon temples are eligible to dwell together in the highest level of the Celestial kingdom. They are kings and priests who will return to the earth with Jesus to reign over the earth. They have a part in the first resurrection. Relatively few people reach the Celestial kingdom and even fewer are exulted to the highest levels.[68]

The belief that most people wind up in the Celestial kingdom appears to contradict D&C 76:109 that says that the inhabitants of the telestial world "were as innumerable as the stars in the firmament of heaven, or as the sand upon the seashore." Logically, the distribution of people among the three heavenly kingdoms would be a pyramid with most in the telestial since most people have not heard the gospel and all men are sinners.

Those who are ignorant of the gospel of Jesus Christ or who reject it must suffer for their sins and so go to hell when they die. Select spirits of the righteous from the Celestial kingdom witness to the spirits in hell. Those who accept the gospel of Jesus Christ (including those who rejected it in life) are freed from hell and dwell in the Terrestrial kingdom. These people receive the presence of Jesus but are not allowed to dwell with the Father. Their glory is less than those of the Celestial kingdom, as the glory of the moon is less than the sun. These people are under the authority of those in the Celestial kingdom but have authority over those in the Telestial kingdom.

The Telestial kingdom is the lowest kingdom of glory. Those who dwell in this kingdom are the wicked people of the earth plus those who repeatedly reject the gospel of Jesus Christ (even after death). These people go to hell when they die and remain there until after the millennial reign of Jesus on earth. The glory of those who dwell in the Telestial kingdom is so marvelous that it surpasses all understanding however, it is less than those who dwell in the other heavenly kingdoms as the stars are less than

---

68   Actually, the Celestial Kingdom will have more souls than any other will, although it is true that fewer will reach exaltation in the highest level.

the sun and moon. These people have not rejected the Holy Ghost, which is the unpardonable sin. The idea that it is possible to reject the gospel of Jesus Christ and not reject the Holy Ghost conflicts with the teachings of the Bible and the books of Mormonism (2 Ne 26:13; D&C 18:32; Mosiah 5:14; Titus 3:5).

Relatively few people remain in hell forever with the devil and his angels. Only those people who "sin against the Holy Ghost" commit the unpardonable sin. This sin against the Holy Ghost is described as rejection of Jesus Christ by those who have perfect knowledge of him (such as the prophets). However, D&C 42:18 also states that those who commit murder commit the unpardonable sin so it appears that there is more than one unpardonable sin. If murder is an unpardonable sin, then most people will be in hell (at least temporarily) since the Bible teaches that those who become angry and wish others ill commit murder in their minds and hearts (Matt 5:21-22).[69]

The Mormon idea of salvation is very different from Christian religions in that virtually everyone is destined to live in a glorious heavenly kingdom after death. Mormons believe that the destiny for most people is not heaven or hell but which heavenly kingdom. Faith in Jesus and repentance prior to death is the dividing point between the Celestial and lower kingdoms. Striving to live a moral life and do good deeds versus living a wicked lifestyle and rejection of the gospel of Jesus Christ is the dividing point between the Terrestrial and Telestial kingdoms. Mormons seek to inhabit the highest levels of the Celestial kingdom based on faith in Jesus, repentance, baptism, receiving the Holy Ghost by the laying on of hands, rites of purification and endowment with wisdom, following God's commands and being married or sealed in a Mormon temple.

Foreordination is an important part of being exalted to the

---

69   There are exceptions to every rule but, in most cases, even murderers will eventually gain a measure of salvation in the Telestial kingdom after paying for their sins in hell.

highest levels of the Celestial kingdom. Foreordination is the discovery of God's plans and obedience to such revelation by each person. Mormons discover God's plans during their teen years in a temple rite called an endowment. An ordained Patriarch declares the person's lineage from a tribe of Israel or their adoption into a tribe of Israel. The Patriarch then gives guidance to the person regarding God's plans for them based on what is said in the blessing he gives. This endowment of divine knowledge can also come directly to Mormons as they draw closer to God and feel driven to serve him in some way.

SALVATION VERSUS EXALTATION

Mormons believe that everyone had a pre-mortal existence as spirit children who lived with God the Father. In order for us to progress and become exalted beings like him, we had to become human and experience separation in order to prove our obedience. After life on earth ends, each of us will be judged and rewarded according to the extent of our faith and obedience. One problem with this view is that the pre-mortal life with God the Father will be taken away for those judged to inhabit the Terrestrial or Telestial kingdoms. Their final existence appears worse than their pre-mortal existence in that they are eternally separated from God despite having glorified bodies. In these cases, human existence appears to result in regression rather than progression since even glorified bodies cannot compensate for the absence of the presence of God.

Exaltation differs from salvation in that it is "the kind of life God lives." Such life is one of perfection in which we can have all knowledge, wisdom and power and become gods and creators. Those who attain the highest level of the Celestial kingdom will be blessed with this level of existence.

Mormon President Joseph Fielding Smith said: *In order to obtain the exaltation we must accept the gospel and all its covenants; and take* upon us the obligations, which the Lord has offered; and walk in the light and the understanding of the truth; and live by every word that proceedeth forth from the mouth of God. (Doctrines of Salvation 2:43).

Mormons believe that faith in Jesus, enduring in good works until death, repentance for sins, obeying God's commandments, receiving certain ordinances—such as baptism, laying of hands by a confirmed member of the LDS Church to receive the Holy Ghost, receiving the Melchizedek Priesthood, receiving the temple endowment and being married for life—are required for exaltation.

The required ordinances include: loving God and our neighbors; searching out our kindred dead and performing baptisms for them; attending Church regularly; family daily prayers and scripture study; teaching the gospel to others and listen and obey the words of the prophets of the Lord.

MORMON RITES

Mormons gather on Sundays in churches to worship and partake in sacraments. Mormon meetings are organized around singing, prayer, instruction, and partaking of the sacrament of bread and water. A traditional Sunday service begins with Sacrament Meeting, in which all members attend. The Bishop and First and Second Counselors lead the meeting and church members give talks on preselected topics. The congregation then breaks into groups based on age and gender. Young children attend Primary, girls attend Young Women, boys attend Young Men, adult women attend Relief Society, and adult men attend Priesthood sessions. In addition to Sunday services, youth in the church attend Mutual, which is joint activities with both the teenage young men and young women, and Seminary, which is daily scripture study during the four years of high school.

There are milestone rituals that begin with baby blessings. A Melchizedek Priesthood holder, who is often the child's father, gives the child a name on earth and for the records of the church. He then pronounces a priesthood blessing on the child. Mormon children are usually baptized when they are eight years old, which is considered the age of accountability. Children of this age are considered old enough to know right from wrong and are able to understand the process of repentance. Persons who are baptized are eligible to receive the gift of the Holy Ghost by the laying on of hands. The Holy Ghost remains as long as the person does not defile the body through sin or substance abuse. This explains why Mormons do not drink alcoholic beverages or coffee.

Worthy boys can be ordained to the offices of deacon, teacher, priest, and bishop as early as 12, 14, 16, and 18, respectively. Male Mormon missionaries hold the Melchizedek Priesthood, which is imparted by ordained elders usually at the age of 18 or 19. All members may receive a Patriarchal Blessing from the district Patriarch, which is a personal blessing imparted to comfort and guide members.

The remaining rites are performed in Mormon temples. High standards of purity are required to enter the temples, so not all Mormons are qualified to enter. To enter, each Mormon must be interviewed by a Bishop (or Bishop's counselor) and a State President or State President's counselor. If approved, a written recommendation is given, which must be renewed every two years.

Proxy baptisms for the dead can be performed by youth as young as 12. This rite is performed for those who died without hearing the gospel. The spirits of the dead have the opportunity to hear the gospel and, if they accept it, they can accept baptism by proxy since they do not have bodies. After baptism, these spirits can also accept the gift of the Holy Ghost by a proxy ordinance conducted in the temple. Baptisms are performed by immersion and by reciting: *(person's name) having been commissioned of Jesus Christ, I baptize you in the name of the Father and of the Son and of the Holy Ghost.* Mormons are baptized for themselves outside the temple but perform proxy baptisms for the dead inside the temples.

The next ordinance for the dead is washing and anointing, which is a purifying ordinance for temple service called the initiatory. A single drop of water and oil is used in this ordinance along with the precise recitation of blessings. The next ordinance is called the temple endowment in which the gift of knowledge, power, and protection from the Lord are imparted. The final temple ordinance is the marriage sealing, in which couples and their families are bound to each other for eternity.

Mormons believe genealogies are important because familial traits both good and bad are passed down through the generations. Thus, knowledge of tendencies towards good and evil is important in personal development. Parents bear a serious responsibility to share their knowledge of God with their children and often do this through family histories. Another reason Mormons believe genealogies are important is because names are extracted from these records and added to the list of people for which baptism can be completed. Church members volunteer their time to be baptized by proxy for those on the list. It is not required to be a relative of the deceased or to have the permission of any living relative. The baptism can be accepted, or not, by the soul of the deceased.[70]

Mormons believe in continuing revelation, so their holy scriptures are not closed. One of their Articles of Faith states that God has revealed and will yet reveal many great and important things pertaining to the Kingdom of God. The revelations that become doctrines come through the Presidents of the Church, or prophets, who are also called apostles.

---

70   1 Peter 4:6 and 1 Corinthians 15:29 address the need for these baptisms.

SUMMARY

A fundamental belief of Mormonism is that Christian churches prior to it were apostate and God had withdrawn His authority from the church. The Church of Christ was thoroughly corrupt due to errors and priest crafts and so needed to be restored (D&C 30:4).

Mormons believe that their church is the only living and true church on earth (D&C 1:30).[71] As recently as 1990, LDS temple ceremonies depicted Protestant ministers as hirelings of Satan (Harrell, 43).

Joseph Smith translated some Bible passages and altered their meanings. He did not work with ancient manuscripts but "simply read the King James Version of the Bible (KJV) and made corrective changes and additions where he felt clarifications were needed (Harrell, 99). There are at least several cases where he revised his own revisions, later discarded his revisions, or marked passages as correct and later changed them. One example is Matthew 24:14, which was changed by Joseph to provide a reference to himself and his work. The KJV version of this verse reads, "And this gospel of the kingdom shall be preached in all the world *for* a witness unto

---

71   This is not to say that Mormons believe other Churches do not teach *any* true doctrines. We acknowledge that other Churches teach many good, worthwhile, and even true doctrines. We do, however, lay a unique claim to being the only Church to possess authentic authority from God to "preach the gospel and administer in the ordinances thereof" (*Article of Faith 5*). This authority was restored literally under the hands of the resurrected John the Baptist, Peter, James, John, and other Old Testament prophets such as Moses, Elias, and Elijah (*see Doctrine & Covenants Sections 29 and 110*).

all nations; and then the end shall come." While in Nauvoo, Joseph Smith said that this passage should read, "the Lord in the last days would commit the keys of the Priesthood *to* a witness over all people" (Ehat and Cook, 365–369). It is interesting to note that this revision does not appear in his earlier translation of Matthew found in JS-M 1:31. While there are references to restorations of various sorts in the *Bible* and *Book of Mormon*, none of them predict a gospel restoration in modern times (Harrell, 60).

Mormons believe in an eternal Godhead of three separate beings that are in perfect unity in attributes and will but not essence. Mormons believe that God the Father was once as man now is, but differ on whether he was like Jesus or ordinary humans in his mortal existence. Humans always existed as intelligences that are not defined and thus are eternal beings. At some point, God the Father created spirit children from the intelligences. Thus, everyone existed as spirits before being given bodies on earth. Humans must experience good and evil in order to advance in knowledge but need a savior to reconcile their sins with God. Jesus is the first-born spirit child of God and has the greatest knowledge of all God's spirit children. Jesus and the Holy Ghost are separate beings but are one in purpose, power, and mind with God the Father.

Mormons believe that God the Father progressed from being a mortal man to a state of perfection "through long periods of growth, development, and progression having passed through all the trials we are now going through." Lorenzo Snow, the fifth President of the LDS Church said, "As man now is, God once was; As God now is, man may be." Therefore, the essence of Mormonism is that human life on earth is a learning experience whereby some will grow and progress to dwell with God. While it is possible to become like him, no one can attain the unity that Jesus and the Holy Ghost have with the Father. This theology is based on a combination of cosmic evolution and achievement through obedience to God's commands. At its core is the desire to become like God, which is the very sin that the *Bible* says caused the angel Lucifer to fall from heaven and become Satan.[72] Current LDS thinking is that humans have the potential to become perfect like God being creators of worlds and having the same glory and power as God (Harrell, 327). While I appreciate that Mormons do not believe that they will rise above God or usurp him, there are aspects to their belief about eventually becoming gods that seem to make such persons God in function, if not in position. The LDS view goes beyond the Biblical view in that it includes creator and ruler aspects of godhood that infer worship by their creation.

> *How you have fallen from heaven*
> *O morning star, son of the dawn!*
> *You have been cast down to the earth,*
> *you who once laid low the nations!*
> *You said in your heart, "I will ascend to heaven;*
> *I will raise my throne above the stars of God;*
> *I will sit enthroned on the mount of the assembly,*
> *on the utmost heights of the sacred mountain will*
> *ascend above the tops of the clouds; I will make myself*
> *like the Most High. But you are brought down to the*
> *grave, to the depths of the pit" (Is 14:12-15).*

Humans have succumbed to the desire to become like God through human effort. Our nature has been corrupted with the desire to discover the hidden things of God and so attain a position

---

72   The goal is not to replace or transcend God, but to progress spiritually to become more like Him (*see* Revelation 21:7). A mortal analogue of this same process occurs in this world as we grow physically, mentally, or otherwise, to become more like our earthly fathers. God, as our Father, will always be above us as our personal God and Patriarch, but this does not mean that as spiritual children of God we can't become more like Him over time. Deification is not an uncommon theme in the Bible. For example, in Romans 8:16-17, Paul refers to us as "heirs" of God with Christ, and in Luke 12:42-44, Christ teaches that God will make the faithful and wise "ruler[s]" over all that he hath." Numerous other Biblical verses reference this theme (Examples include: Matthew 5:48, Luke 6:40, Galatians 4:7, 1 John 3:2, Revelation 3:21.

elevated above mere humanity. This is the same lie that led to the fall of mankind in the Garden of Eden when the devil tempted Eve through the serpent to partake of the forbidden fruit.

> *"You will not surely die," the serpent said to the woman.*
> *"For God knows that when you eat of it your eyes will*
> *be opened, And you will be like God, knowing good and*
> *evil" (Gen 3:4-5).*

A book that describes the development of Mormon Theology is titled **This is My Doctrine, The Development of Mormon Theology** by Charles R. Harrell, PhD who is a Mormon. Dr. Harrell says that:

1. The Bible and Mormon sacred scriptures are Inspired by God but do not reflect consistent and true theology.
2. God's word is not static but subject to change.
3. Sacred scriptures are a product of human culture and therefore revealed truth is imperfect as it is expressed by imperfect humans.
4. Doctrines are beliefs about reality and as such are dynamic and change with time.
5. Scriptures are the word of God but are not literally God's words.
6. Prophets can't always discern between their thoughts and those revealed to them by God.

These premises lead to a fluid belief system in which divine revelations are subject to revision. Holy scriptures contain God's truth but are not the final and inalterable word of God. God reveals truth through "finite and fallible humans, it is never perfect, and therefore never final" (Harrell, viii). It seems to me that this line of thinking leads to unreliable scriptures upon which to base a belief system. The net result is confusing in that scriptures are simultaneously inspired, authoritative, and imperfect and fallacious as they represent the limited understanding of the revelators and the corrupting influence of their cultures. While there are conservative Mormons who would view their scriptures as infallible, Harrell describes in great detail the many contradictions and alterations of scriptures by Joseph Smith and other LDS leaders to change the meaning of their previous revelations to fit their later beliefs. This results in an evolution of doctrines that are revised and sometimes completely changed from previously held beliefs. This also explains why *The Book of Mormon* reflects doctrines more closely aligned to 19th century Protestantism than later Mormon scriptures found in *The Doctrines and Covenants* and *Pearl of Great Price*. Examples of this evolution of doctrine are presented in the following table.

Doctrine	Book Of Mormon	Later Revelations
Nature of God	Trinitarian (2Ne 32:21; Morm 7:7)	Plurality of Gods united in purpose (Abr 4:1–3)
Eternal Perfection of God	Unchangeable (Moro 8:18)	God the Father was once as man now is (D&C 130:22;)
The Nature of Jesus	Jesus is Son of God who takes on the image of man in flesh (Mos 7:27); 2Ne 25:12; 3Ne 1:14)	Jesus is biological Son of God the Father (D&C 93:12–14)
Holy Ghost	Impersonal mind, power or influence of Father & Son (2Ne 32:5;Alma 34:38)	Holy Ghost is a spirit person who is God along with God the Father and God the Son (D&C 130:22)
How To Enter Heaven	Faith or faith plus repentance and enduring to the end. Only a few will be saved (3Ne 27:33; Alma 7:14)	Everyone will go to one of three heavenly kingdoms and be glorified except for demons and a relative few humans known as the sons of perdition(D&C 76:43–44)
Salvation Of The Dead	Dead went either to heaven or hell (Alma 34:34–35; 40:12–26; Mosiah 16:11)	Spirits of dead people in hell can go to heaven if they accept the gospel preached by the spirits of righteous dead (D&C 76:72–76)

The revelations of Joseph Smith and LDS leaders vary significantly over time and can be grouped into roughly three periods: Early (1828–1835), Kirtland and Nauvoo (1835–1844), and Later (mid-1800s after Joseph Smith). Most of the key Mormon doctrines that distinguish it from other Christian faiths are not mentioned in *The Book of Mormon* or *Book of Commandments*, which is a precursor to *The Doctrines and Covenants*. Some of these are listed below:

1. Melchizedek and Aaronic Priesthoods
2. Temple endowment
3. Eternal marriage
4. Three heavenly kingdoms
5. Baptisms for the dead
6. Humans are spirit offspring of heavenly parents
7. Satan as a spirit child of God the Father

The alteration of previous scriptures and the revelations of new concepts that change, reverse, or add new layers of complexity typically resulted in the departure of significant numbers of Smith's followers (Shipps, 296). The LDS Church has never published an official exposition on Mormon doctrines and remains "a-theological...without a church-sanctioned, church-approved, or even church-encouraged systematic theology" (Harrel, 1).

Joseph Smith became a mason and his teachings regarding temple worship, pre-existence, and the cosmos resonate with ideas found in Free Masonry, the Apocrypha, and Jewish Midrash that he studied during this time (Harrell, 22).

Joseph Smith initially saw his mission as a "restorer of lost truths through the translation of ancient records, particularly the *Book of Mormon*" (Harrell, 101). After the publication of the *Book of Mormon*, Joseph told David Whitmer that he had completed the work God had given him except to preach the gospel.[73] He promised to bring forth translations of other ancient records of the gospel that have been hidden because of wickedness (D&C 6:26). However, he never did this and "after 1836 changed his vocation from a restorer of ancient records to a builder of God's kingdom on earth (Harrell, 102).

Given the history of shifting doctrines and evolutionary revelations by Mormon leaders, it is apparent that there is a great deal of flexibility in what LDS members can choose to believe. Members are expected to be supportive of their leaders and the goals of the Church. The LDS Church expects its members to be temple worthy and follow a few core beliefs:

1. God exists;
2. Jesus is the redeemer;
3. Restoration of the Church, and
4. The Church continues to be guided by a living prophet.

LDS members consider themselves to be further enlightened in comparison to other Christians who limit themselves to the *Bible*. Instead of being bound to consistent scriptural texts to validate beliefs, many LDS have relied on "the rational appeal or resonance of Mormon theology" to provide convincing evidence of its truthfulness (Harrell, 502). This is to say that reason defines truth. Scriptural validation is not necessary to support beliefs and scriptural contradictions to beliefs do not falsify them (Harrell, 503). Therefore, scriptural validation becomes secondary rather than a primary support for LDS beliefs. This line of thinking certainly helps to resolve the plethora of problems with Mormon scriptures and doctrines. However, the doctrinal evolution of this line of thinking ultimately frees itself from the constraints of scriptures. This results in truth being defined by prophetic

---

73   *Book of Commandments*, 4:2.

revelations and the reasoning of man. As we have seen, Joseph Smith taught that a prophet couldn't be sure that revelations are accurate because they are prone to be corrupted by human reasoning.

A confounding conundrum...

BOOK REVIEW REQUEST

Thank you for taking your valuable time to read my book. I hope you enjoyed reading it as much as I enjoyed writing it. What did you think? I want to know. I would appreciate if you would take a few minutes to write a review for this book on Amazon.com. Thank you in advance for taking the time to respond. I look forward to reading your review.

REFERENCES

Ari D Bruening and David L. Paulsen. *The Development of the Mormon Understanding of God: Early Mormon Modalism and Other Myths,* FARMS Review: vol.13, no.2, (2001):109–169

Bennett, Robert R. *Horses in the Book of Mormon,* Neal A. Maxwell Institute for Religious Scholarship. Last updated August 2000. http://maxwellinstitute.byu.edu/publications/transcripts/?id=129

Cowdrey, Wayne L., Howard A. Davis and Arthur Vanick. *Who Really Wrote The Book Of Mormon?* Concordia Publishing House. 2005.

Ehat, Andrew F. and Lyndon W. Cook, eds. *The Words of Joseph Smith: The Contemporary Accounts of the Nauvoo Discourses of the Prophet Joseph Smith,* Provo, Utah: BYU Religious Studies Center, 1980.

FAIRMormon. Book of Abraham. http://en.fairmormon.org/Book of Abraham/Joseph Smith Papyri

Gospel Principles. Salt Lake City; Church of Jesus Christ of Latter-day Saints, 1979.

Harrell, Charles R. *This Is My Doctrine, The Development of Mormon Theology.* Gregg Kofford Books. 2011

"Origin of *The Book of Mormon,*" *Sewickley, PA Herald,* 23 November 1912.

Rhodes, Michael D. *Teaching the Book of Abraham Facsimiles. The Religious Educator: Perspectives on the Restored Gospel,* Vol. 4, No. 2 (2003): 115–123.

Scofield, C. I. (ed.) *The New Scofield Study Bible: New International Version.* Copyright 1984 by the International Bible Society.

Used by permission of the Oxford University Press. All rights reserved.

Shipps, Jan. *Mormonism: The Story of a New Religious Tradition.* Urbana: University of Illinois Press, 1987.

Smith, Joseph Fielding. *Doctrines of Salvation: Compiled Sermons of Joseph Fielding Smith.* Compiled by Bruce R McConkie. 3 Vols. Salt Lake City: Bookcraft, 1954–1956.

The Proclamation to the World on the Family. President Gordon B. Hinckley, as part of his message at the General Relief Society Meeting held September 23, 1995, in Salt Lake City, Utah. http://www.lds.org/topics/family-proclamation

AUTHOR'S NOTE

My greatest credential is my daily and systematic study of the Bible over the past thirty plus years. My motivation for doing this comes from a deep love and commitment I have to experience ever more of the transforming presence of God in my life. The foundation for this motivation is a spiritual birth that has fundamentally changed me. Prior to this birth, there was only "I," but since then there is always "we." Over the years, my knowledge and experience of God have increased because of regular Bible study, prayer, and interaction with other believers. I have been a deacon, taught Sunday School classes and small groups, spoken in churches and conventions as a Gideon, and have performed many good deeds that I would never have considered by myself. I have learned that these credentials or accomplishments are worthless unless they originate from and are an expression of the love I have for God. Indeed, these very same actions can become a hindrance in that the status, accomplishments, and praise of others can be the motivation rather than an expression of love.

In America, copies of the Bible are plentiful, but still few have read it. Therefore, most people do not know what it says. We have put our trust in theologians or religious leaders, which has resulted in the popular belief that the Bible is hard to understand due to many interpretations, or that it contains contradictions or myths. It is not necessary to have a theological degree or training to understand the Bible. The essentials are a born-again faith in

Jesus Christ and disciplined study. Seek the advice and counsel of theologians, Christian books, and other believers, but do not be bound by them. Let the Bible always rule in seeking God's message and perspective.

INDEX